Ballistic Basics

A writer's primer on firearms and the forensics that track them

by
J. Gunnar Grey

δ

Dingbat Publishing
Humble, Texas

Ballistic Basics

Ballistic Basics: A writer's primer on firearms and the forensics that track them
Copyright © 2012 by J. Gunnar Grey
ISBN 978-1475104707

Cover design by Dingbat Publishing
Cover photo: Close-up of an M9 semi-auto pistol, taken by Cpl. Kurt Fredrickson.

This publication is designed to provide accurate and authoritative information in regard to the subject matter covered. It does not claim to be perfect. It is sold with the understanding that the sale does not engage the Publisher in any manner for the rendering of professional services to the buyer.

Foreword

This book was designed to provide some basic information on firearms and ballistics for writers who might not have personal experience or who don't trust the television shows to get it right. However, the information may also be of interest to other readers as well as fans of true crime, especially those who like to delve into the history of it all.

Ballistic Basics covers how a gun works and how those workings gave rise to forensic ballistics. It also includes a description of the various categories of civilian firearms, a timeline of firearm and ballistics development for historical writers, and what happens in a ballistic forensics lab. A few historical cases are discussed, showcasing the changes in criminal investigations and court cases as the science developed during the 20th century. Finally, there's a brief history of police departments and police casualties in the line of duty, written by a friend who prefers to remain kinda anonymous, "Scotty."

These sections don't need to be read in any particular order, and some of the arranging depended upon when an idea struck me rather than any form of logic. However, the first section, "The theory behind forensic ballistics," which began as a post on my blog, Mysteries and Histories (the1940mysterywriter.com), can be considered a basic primer for writerly firearms, with everything that follows leading off from that point. Might be a good idea to start there.

No basic primer on any subject can cover all its aspects, so allow me to apologize in advance for any omissions.

Gunnar

The theory behind forensic ballistics

To understand the science of forensic ballistics, it helps to understand a) how a round of ammunition is constructed, b) how a gun barrel is manufactured, and c) how a gun works.

a) The modern *cartridge* (another name for a round of ammunition) consists of a cylindrical tube with a sealed base, called a shell casing and usually made from brass, that's filled with gunpowder and plugged shut on the open end with a bullet.

BULLET

Figure 1
Anatomy of a cartridge.

Figure 2
Fired centerfire casing.

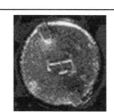

Figure 3
Fired rimfire casing.

The base includes a primary explosive charge (the *primer*), either rolled into the casing's edge (*rimfire* ammunition) or enclosed within a tiny metal cup called a percussion cap, which is then inserted into a little recess in the brass casing (*centerfire*). There's a flash hole between the primer and the gunpowder, so when one goes off, the other follows a millisecond later. Some bullets are made slightly larger than the barrel of the intended gun; some are made slightly smaller. (More on this in a bit.)

b) Most gun barrels are manufactured from solid metal rods. Such a rod is first bored out and smoothed to a precise diameter, then it's *rifled* with a machine carving tool, etching a pattern of spiral *grooves* into the barrel's interior, with raised areas called *lands* between the grooves. Gun barrels can also be forged over mandrels containing a reverse image of the rifling desired by the manufacturer. This rifling forces the bullet to whirl or spin about an axis, stabilizing its flight and improving the shooter's ability to aim.

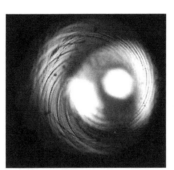

Figure 4
Rifling inside Remington .35 caliber barrel.

Note that the tools used in the boring and rifling processes are worn down a bit by each successive rod that's transformed into a gun barrel. At the microscopic level, therefore, no two gun barrels are precisely the same — just like fingerprints. (And no, you can't say that about DNA, because identical twins have identical DNA. But their fingerprints will be slightly different, due to scars from paper cuts and such.)

c) When a gun's trigger is pulled, the *firing pin* strikes the primer, setting off the explosive. This in turn ignites the gunpowder, which detonates in a controlled explosion, heats the bullet to a semi-liquid state, and hurls it through the barrel into flight. Bullets that are slightly smaller than the barrel flare out and enlarge to fill the space; those that are slightly larger are squeezed to fit. In both instances, the bullet's semi-liquid metal engages the rifling and is permanently marked by the interaction as it cools back to a solid form.

For the gun to be fired a second time (or the chamber, in the case of a revolver), the now hot and empty *brass casing* must be removed. Some guns rely upon the explosion's gasses to propel the brass from the firing chamber, called the *breech*; others use an *extractor* mechanism, which may include an *ejector,* as well. Many revolvers with *swing-out cylinders* have a manual ejector system, where the shooter can push in a rod on the cylinder's front and force the casings from all the chambers at one time. Finally, many other revolvers require the shooter to remove the casings from the barrel and reload manually. While this method may seem simplistic, it has the undeniable benefit that there's less to potentially go wrong.

This sequence of events gives the forensic ballistics expert two potential evidentiary items at the scene of a shooting: the bullet and the ejected brass casing. The bullet will carry *striations* from the barrel's rifling. The casing will be marked by the firing pin, any imperfections on the firing chamber's *breech face,* and the individual gun's ejector mechanism. These markings can first identify the type of weapon used in the shooting, and later confirm or disprove that a particular weapon fired the bullet in question.

If a bullet strikes a hard surface (a brick wall, for example, or a bone), it can be smashed into a mis-shapen lump, destroying or altering the marks left by the barrel's rifling. Therefore the brass casing can be

more valuable for identifying a murder weapon, particularly if the manufacturing process left small
imperfections or tool marks on the gun's breech, firing
mechanism, or ejector. For this reason, criminals often
try to collect and carry off expended shell casings after
committing a crime, or they fire the gun through a
paper bag, which camouflages the gun until it's fired
and hopefully contains the casings that would otherwise be hurled about. Of course, if the paper bag is
blasted apart, he's back to picking up shell casings.

Firearms and ballistics timeline

9th century: *Gunpowder* was invented in China by alchemists searching for an elixir of immortality, which is ironic considering it's often used by murderers as an elixir of death.

10th century: The first *firearm* was invented in China, too, as part of the ongoing defense against the encroaching Mongol hordes along the northern Chinese border. (They built the Great Wall of China for the same reason, starting around 50 BC and continuing for more than twelve centuries.) These early weapons were crude but generally effective, such as the fire-spear, a bamboo pipe filled with shrapnel and gunpowder, used as a sort of combination flame-thrower and grenade launcher.

Figure 5
Tenth century Dunhuang fire-spear and grenade launcher.

11

12th century: The Chinese proved under attack to be quick learners. Before the end of the century, they'd altered the gunpowder mix to turn it from a raw explosive to an explosive propellant. They'd also changed their shrapnel bits to solid cannonballs, and instead of mounting bamboo pipes on the ends of spears, they invented the metal barrel. Thus was created the first cannon, and the invention spread through the Middle East to Europe, ironically driven mainly by the Mongols after they overran China.

14th century: Early artillery arrived in the Middle East, brought by invading Mongols. Those guys got around.

14th century: Not long after, the first field artillery arrived in Europe. By the 1340s, the English army was equipped with *ribauldequins,* a sort of early organ gun, fielded by Edward III in France during the Hundred Years War. These ribauldis had multiple small barrels, usually nine to twelve of them, all bound together into one field piece. The barrels pointed either straight ahead as a group or spread out in a fan formation; drawings by Leonardo da Vinci show both patterns. All the barrels went off together, creating a true mur-dering-piece blast of lead against enemy pikemen, archers, and foot soldiers.

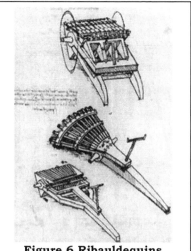

Figure 6 Ribauldequins drawn by Leonardo da Vinci.

14th century: Near the end of the century, a clever inventor shrank the cannon and put a handle on it, creating the first smooth-bore pistol. Despite the battlefield artillery, killing continued to be up close and personal.

15th century: Modern infantry was invented when the Ottoman Empire outfitted their foot soldiers with firearms as standard procedure. It took a while for new tactics to catch on, though.

16th century: August Kotter, a Nuremberg armorer, took a rough idea from the end of the 15th century and improved it, creating the first truly *rifled barrel*. Engraving grooves into a barrel's interior forced the projectile to spin, making its flight more stable and improving the gunner's aim. Although Kotter didn't realize it at the time, his improvement also made individual firearms traceable.

17th century: Between 1610 and 1615, the *flintlock* mechanism was developed by Marin le Bourgeoys, a French painter and inventor in the employ of Louis XIII. As he invented it, the flintlock had a literal piece

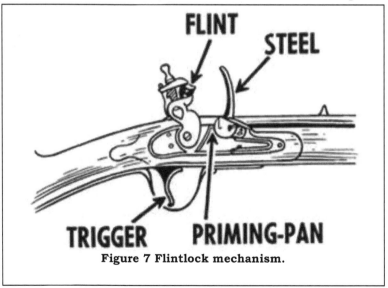

Figure 7 Flintlock mechanism.

of flint locked into the hammer, intended to strike a spark and set off the primer when the trigger was pulled. The expression "flash in the pan" originated with flintlocks and referred to a misfire where the primer exploded but didn't ignite the gunpowder, causing a bang and cloud of smoke around the flintlock's chamber, but very little else. The flintlock's "half-cocked" position served as a sort of safety, as the gun wasn't supposed to "go off" from there. Flintlock mechanisms were widely used for two centuries in all sorts of firearms, including pistols, rifles, field artillery, and naval cannons.

18th century: Benjamin Robins, an English mathematics teacher, applied Newtonian physics to gunnery and realized that an elongated bullet or cannonball would cut through the air more efficiently and still retain the speed and punch of a round one. His findings, published as *New Principles in Gunnery* in 1742, revolutionized firearms and later, military science.

Note: After this point in history, weaponry innovations came so thick and fast, it's difficult now to separate out the facts and determine who actually invented what. There are competing claims for development of fulminate primers, percussion caps, and various other inventions, some of which were settled by lawsuit and others which haven't been settled yet.

19th century:
1807: Not until this point did someone get sufficiently tired of the flintlock's misfiring to do something constructive about it. And actually, what bothered the Reverend Alexander Forsyth wasn't the misfiring; it was the rising smoke from his fowler's powder pan that alerted sitting birds he was about to shoot them. The good reverend invented a *concussion primer* based upon fulminate of mercury, eliminating that first puff

of smoke as well as the sometimes seconds-long delay between when the shooter pulled the trigger and when the flintlock actually fired. Seven years later, the first metallic *percussion cap* appeared on the firearms market.

1835: The first recorded crime solved through *forensic ballistics* seems to have occurred when a servant was suspected of murdering his employer. A Bow Street Runner, Henry Goddard, compared the homemade lead projectile used in the shooting with the bullet mold owned by the servant, and confirmed their relationship through markings on both. He also traced the paper patch, inserted into the muzzle-loading gun between the powder and the ball, as having been torn from a newspaper found in the servant's quarters.

1836: Samuel Colt, a manufacturer in Paterson, NJ, patented his *single-action* revolver model. Although similar revolvers existed as far back as 1597 (a revolving arquebus) and early 1700s (the Puckle gun), and although Colt added little to the revolver's actual design, he developed the manufacturing processes that allowed for mass production. Back in the Old West, it was a common truism that Abe Lincoln might have freed all men, but Sam Colt made them equal.

Figure 8 1840 ad for 1836 Colt revolver.

15

1845: Although an *integrated cartridge* held together with paper was patented in 1812, the *full metal cartridge* didn't appear until about this point. Called the ".22 Bulleted Breech Cap," or .22 BB (no relation to the other type of BB), it attached a round ball to a rimfire casing. Integrated centerfire cartridges utilizing metallic priming caps appeared not long after.

1850s: Robert Adams, who worked for a London manufacturer, invented the *double-action* revolver, where one pull of the trigger cocked the hammer, turned the cylinder so the next round entered the firing chamber, and released the hammer, firing the shot. It speeded up the rate of fire over the old single-action revolvers but the long, resistant trigger pull tended to damage the shooter's accuracy. Colt's manufacturing processes had not yet crossed the ocean, and so the five-shooter, centerfire Adams revolvers were individually handmade. Parts could not always be swapped about between different guns and it was a toss-up over whether the ability to fire faster outweighed the Adams revolver's inherent disadvantages. A number of British soldiers carrying them in the Crimean War owed their lives to the rapid rate of fire, but American sharpshooters were pickier.

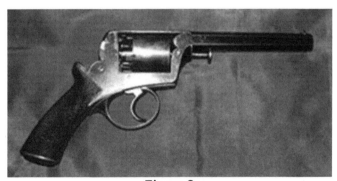

Figure 9
1854 Adams revolver.

1863: During the Civil War, Confederate General Stonewall Jackson died after taking gunfire during the Battle of Chancellorsville. The bullets were removed and examination showed them to be .67-caliber rounds that could only have come from the nearby 18th North Carolina Infantry Regiment; Union forces used .58-caliber Minié rounds, shown below. Jackson was a victim of not-so-friendly fire and showed it was possible to determine the specific type of firearm used in a shooting. In 1864, the Union followed a similar procedure to determine that General John Sedgwick was killed by a Confederate sniper firing a British-made Whitworth rifle.

Figure 10 Civil War era Minié bullets.

1884: Originally gunpowder was called *black powder* and it created a ton of smoke on historic battlefields, making it difficult to find the enemy, much less kill him. In 1884 a French chemist, Paul Vielle, tinkered with black powder's chemical mixture and created a different blend, one with higher power and lower explosive volatility (safer). It would fire even when wet, needed less powder per round of ammunition, and created far less smoke. Vielle's *smokeless gunpowder* changed firearm manufacturing yet again, making possible thousand-meter shots. From up-close-and-personal, killing once again became long-distance death affairs.

1885: German firearms engineer Ferdinand Ritter von

Mannlicher introduced his design for a weapon that didn't require cocking between shots. He's credited with inventing the *semi-automatic* and opening the pathway for *full automatic* weapons.

1886: Since Paul Vielle's smokeless powder made lead bullets and the weapons that fired them obsolete, a team of French soldiers and armorers invented the *Lebel rifle,* the first modern infantry firearm. With a *bolt-action,* tubular *magazine, metal-jacketed* bullets, smokeless powder, and accuracy over about a quarter mile, the Lebel rifle saw much action in the First World War. In a clear indication of the arms race then underway, Germany and Austria adopted similar weapons within two years.

1889: French criminologist Alexandre Lacassagne tried to match a fired bullet to an individual gun based on barrel *striations.* This seems to be the first time an investigator took that obvious next step.

1896: Although inventers had been trying to make revolvers as easy and quick to reload as semi-autos for years, only in the 1890s was the *moon clip* or basic *speedloader* perfected. They became better known in the first decade of the 20th century and very popular with soldiers in World War I trenches, especially those firing revolvers against enemy machine gun positions.

1897: A Virginia appellate court allowed testimony regarding the similarities between a bullet from a crime scene and a test-fired one, based upon weight.

1898: A Berlin chemist known as "the German Sherlock Holmes," Paul Jeserich, used *microphotography* to trace a fired bullet back to a specific weapon. Although others had tried it, he succeeded, making this an important year for forensic ballistics.
20th century:

1900: Dr. Albert Llewellyn Hall published "The Missile and the Weapon" in the *Buffalo Medical Journal,* which even in those days of wild-and-woolly scientific expansion seems an unusual match. The paper not only covered the systematic measurement of bullet striations, but also how firing a weapon alters it and how gunpowder *residue* accumulates in the barrel.

1907: In a confusing case involving the U.S. Army and a riot in the Texas border town of Brownsville, the investigation covered not only the bullets and suspected rifles, but also the collected cartridge casings. As well, the detailed written report, while not unusual for the military, was a first for forensic science.

1912: Victor Balthazard, professor of forensic medicine at the Sarbonne, used a series of photographic enlargements to *individuate* a fired bullet to a specific gun with scientific accuracy. His examination included not only the bullet striations, but also the shell casing markings from the firing pin, breech facing, extractor, and ejector — the same techniques used by modern ballistic experts today.

1916–25: Charles E. Waite began compiling *manufacturers' data* (lands and grooves, *twist rate and direction*, rimfire or centerfire, ejector and extractor mechanisms if applicable, etc.) from various firearms into the first guidebook for ballistic forensics investigators. For the first time, a detective could match a fired bullet to a firearm variety without performing his own testing.

1920s: After an innocent farmhand came within hours of execution due to outrageous ballistics "expert testimony," Charles Waite, Calvin Goddard (no relation to Henry Goddard, discussed earlier), Phillip O. Gravelle, and John H. Fisher invented the *comparison microscope.* It's basically two microscopes joined at the eyepiece, allowing an examiner to directly compare the striations on two different bullets to ascertain if they were fired by the same gun. The comparison microscope remains a standard tool of modern forensic ballistics.

1925: Dr. (later Sir) Sydney Smith of New Zealand and the University of Edinburgh arrived in Cairo in 1917 as a medico-legal expert to the Egyptian Ministry of Justice. Egypt was in political turmoil at the time; attacks and assassinations were common, and most of them involved gunfire. An early expert on the interactions between bullets and bodies, Dr. Smith systematically collected fired bullets and casings from crime scenes, building an array of data unprecedented on the subject. His *Textbook of Forensic Medicine* became an authoritative source through multiple printings although it was controversial when first published in 1925 because it insisted upon classifying ballistics as a science.

1925: The *Saturday Evening Post* published a two-part article entitled "Fingerprinting Bullets — The Silent Witness." Forensic ballistics hit the big time for the first time. All of you readers who watch those *CSI* type shows, remember: there's nothing new under the sun.

1926: The death sentences of Nicola Sacco and Bartolomeo Vanzetti were upheld when the comparison microscope proved the bullets that killed security guards Frederick Parmenter and Alessandro Berardelli were fired by Sacco's revolver. Upon re-examination in 1961 and 1983, these findings were confirmed, and claims that Sacco and Vanzetti were tried for their anarchist politics rather than their crime were discredited.

1929: Calvin Goddard test-fired every Thompson *submachine gun* in the Chicago police department and compared them with the evidence recovered from the St. Valentine's Day Massacre crime scene. He proved that, although the murderers wore police uniforms, no Thompson related to the PD fired the bullets that killed seven Chicago mobsters.

Figure 11
Thompson submachine gun, a/k/a tommy gun.

1934–1935: Several major works on forensic ballistics were written in these years, indicating the field's level of acceptance amongst law enforcement and judicial departments. In London in 1934, Major Sir Gerald Burrard published *The Identification of Firearms and Forensic Ballistics,* which included discussions of some famous cases in the United Kingdom. In the U.S. in 1935, Major Julian S. Hatcher of the U.S. Army Ordnance Corps published *Textbook of Firearms Investigation, Identification and Evidence,* which was widely used by examiners in the field. Finally, Jack D. and Charles O. Gunther, respectively a New York attorney and a mathematics professor and lieutenant-colonel in the U.S. Army Ordnance Corps Reserve, wrote *The Identification of Firearms from Ammunition Fired Therein.* The concept of forensic ballistics as a science was now widely accepted.

1969: The Association of Firearm and Tool Mark Examiners was organized.

1974: In another of those odd matchups, scientists employed by Aerospace Corporation developed a technique for detecting gunshot residue using scanning electron microscopy with electron dispersive X-rays (SEMEDX). No matter how helpful the technique, that's a mouthful to say.

1975: The FBI began offering training courses for firearm examiners and ballistics experts.

1991–92: Separate automated imaging systems, designed to catalog striations on bullets and marks on shell casings recovered from crime scenes, were developed first in Canada and then in the United States. Walsh Automation, Inc., of Montreal led the way with their Integrated Ballistics Identification System (IBIS), which was adopted by the U.S. Bureau of Alcohol, Tobacco, and Firearms (ATF). The following year, the U.S. Federal Bureau of Investigations (FBI) working with Mnemonic Systems, Inc., of Washington, brought out DRUGFIRE, giving everyone a choice of snappy acronyms. In 1999, the two competing U.S. government bureaus allowed an exchange of data between the two systems. Firearms used in multiple crimes could now be easily tracked across state and even international borders.

Types of firearms and ammunition

Broadly speaking, there are only two types of firearms: those fired with one hand (handguns) and those fired from the shoulder with both hands (long guns). These simplistic categories, however, subdivide into several additional branches.

Handguns

Handguns or pistols are categorized by the type of *feeding mechanism* employed — by what gets the cartridge to the firing chamber.

Revolvers

A revolver has a rotating *cylinder*. The chambers are arranged in a circle within this cylinder, which rotates around a central axis and places each successive cartridge in front of the firing mechanism. Generally there's between five and nine chambers in a revolver's cylinder, with six being the classic number (a "six-shooter").

Some revolvers must be cocked before each shot (a *single-action* revolver). Pulling

Figure 12
Bowen 500 Lindbaugh revolver.

back the hammer rotates the cylinder and brings the next round to bear. Some single-action revolvers don't include a *safety catch,* relying upon the hammer remaining un-cocked to prevent accidental discharges; these are mainly older or less expensive weapons. Most modern single-action revolvers include a safety catch of some sort, even if it is somewhat redundant.

Figure 13
Revolver loaded with three rounds and the cylinder open.

Other revolvers only need for the hammer to be cocked once (*double-action*). The cylinder rotates and brings the next cartridge into the firing chamber with each trigger pull, without the need to cock the hammer in between shots. The downside to this otherwise very handy feature is that the trigger pull's double duty tends to make for a long, hard pull indeed, requiring more strength from the shooter's hand. It's also tougher to hold the revolver steady while pulling a double-action's trigger, which tends to detract from the shooter's accuracy. Modern double-action revolvers generally have a safety catch that prevents the gun from being fired accidentally. As well, many double-action revolvers can be switched to a single-action mode simply by cocking the hammer, easing the pressure on the trigger pull.

Older revolvers require the shooter to open the cylinder, manually remove the spent shell casings, and then push a fresh cartridge into each chamber. More modern revolvers will eject the casings, but the shooter must still reload manually. To hurry up that operation, knowledgeable shooters, or those whose lives may depend upon their ability to fire quickly (police officers or PIs), use *moon clips* or *speedloaders,* which are a sort of magazine for revolvers. It's a metal disc that securely holds as many rounds as the revolver can load at one time. The shooter just dumps out the spent casings, drops a prepared speedloader into place, closes the cylinder, and she's back in business. Note that not all revolvers can utilize speedloaders. While it takes less than a minute to reload a revolver without one, the difference in time can determine the winner in a firefight.

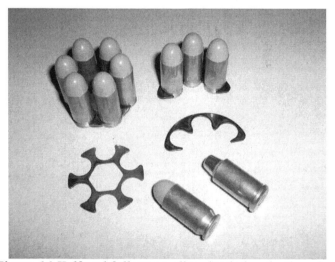

Figure 14 Half and full moon clips, loaded and otherwise.

Autoloaders

An *autoloading* pistol feeds the next bullet into the firing chamber as the preceding one is fired, with no need for the shooter to cock the hammer or operate the *slide*. A *semi-auto* requires a pull of the trigger between shots and it ejects the spent shell casing to the side, up and out.

Figure 15 M14 target practice aboard USS *Ronald Reagan*, with spent shell casing flying.

These pistols generally have a box-shaped *magazine* that inserts into the handle or grip, holding six to a dozen rounds; some semi-autos can utilize *double-stack* magazines holding twice the usual number. The Hollywood image of two magazines taped end-to-end generally doesn't work with a semi-auto pistol, because mags are designed to fit flush against the pistol's grip, leaving no room for the tape, which could actually be scraped off by the act of inserting the upper mag.

When a magazine is empty, the shooter works a release catch that ejects the mag from the *grip*; he can replace it with a full one or stop to insert fresh cartridges into the same one before ramming it back into place. In a firefight, emptied magazines are often considered expendable, dropped and forgotten in the heat of the action. But this can be a mistake, because some mags mark the bullet and shell casing in a forensically traceable manner. (More on this in the section on ballistics examinations.)

Figure 16 Loading a fresh magazine into an M9 pistol aboard the USS *Boxer*.

Because magazines are spring-loaded, it takes some finger strength to push the bullets in and it requires more time to reload a semi-auto magazine than a revolver. At the same time, almost all magazines hold more rounds than almost all revolvers, so more shots can be fired before there's a need to reload. There's an audible *click* when the magazine locks home in the grip. The shooter then pulls back the slide, on top of the semi-auto, to work the uppermost cartridge into the firing chamber and cock the hammer; he's then ready to resume firing.

A *fully automatic* weapon (*assault* or *machine* pistol) can fire multiple rounds with one pull, continuing to fire as long as the shooter holds the trigger. Historical machine pistols usually have only two settings, semi-auto or full auto fire. Modern ones may include a sort of middle position, which fires typically three shots with one trigger pull. This gives the advantage of full automatic fire without emptying the shooter's magazine in one hit. Because machine pistols rip through ammunition at incredible speed, firing eight to twenty rounds *per second,* they tend to be designed with larger magazines, holding more rounds than semi-autos, or to have aftermarket jumbo-size magazines designed to fit them. These are sometimes shaped like a drum instead of a box, but not all machine pistols can use these. There's no time for the shooter to recover between fully automatic shots, so machine pistols also tend to recoil or "kick" more than semi-autos, although they load and otherwise fire in the same manner.

Long guns

Modern firearms designed to be fired from the shoulder with both hands are also divided into two categories. Here, the line of departure is the type of ammunition and how it interacts with the barrel.

Rifles

A modern *rifle* fires an *integrated* metal cartridge encasing a single bullet, using a rifled barrel (never a smoothbore except for historical reenactment weapons). Some of the simplest rifles are *single-shot,* meaning the shooter must reload and cock the hammer after firing each round. Some rifles are *double-barrelled,* firing one side or the other or both at the same time. But by far the largest percentage of modern rifles are like elongated semi-auto pistols: one barrel, magazine-fed, firing a single bullet each time the trigger is pulled, ejecting spent casings up and out automatically, and not requiring the hammer to be cocked between shots.

The average rifle fires its bullet at a significantly higher velocity than a handgun, meaning gravity has less time to act on the projectile and it therefore travels farther and straighter. In short, a rifle will typically have a much greater *field of fire* than a pistol and be more accurate, as well. Of course there are exceptions to this rule of thumb, and the actual results achieved will vary by make, model, firearm caliber, and ammunition used. But on average, a rifle will outshoot a pistol every time.

One interesting type of rifle, called the *bullpup,* places the firing chamber behind the trigger, where the shoulder stock is located on a traditional rifle. This arrangement makes the bullpup look rather like an oversized semi-auto pistol, and indeed many of them use pistol grips plus a sort of blunt stock that the shooter

Figure 17 P90 bullpup carried by Cypriot National Guardsman. The thing on top is the magazine.

butts up against her shoulder. To accommo-date left-handed shooters, some bullpups can be reconfigured so they eject to the left side instead of the right (the Steyr AUG), while others eject forward (the FN F2000 and the Kel-Tec 7.62mm RFB) or downward (military full-auto FN P90 or civilian semi-auto FN PS90).

Figure 18 Combat-ready SA80 bullpup assault rifle. Note how the pistol grip is in front of the magazine, and instead of a rifle stock, there's a concave butt plate to tuck into the shoulder.

Shotguns

The other variety of long gun, the *shotgun,* is separated out from all other firearms, because here is where ballistic forensics goes a bit off the rails. See, shotguns are different from every other type of firearm out there.

A shotgun fires an integrated plastic (modern) or cardboard (historic) casing called a *shell,* filled with *pellets* as well as the primer and gunpowder to make them fly. The shell is designed to come apart in the barrel, retaining or ejecting the casing and propelling the pellets and *wadding material* into individual flight. Once past the barrel's mouth, the pellets spread out, covering a significantly wider stretch of territory than either a handgun or rifle, but at a lower velocity and therefore shorter range.

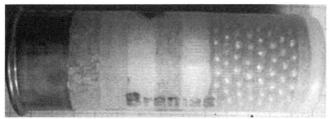

Figure 19 Shotgun shell with transparent casing, showing the layers of wadding and gunpowder, and 12-gauge shot.

The earliest and simplest shotguns fold or *break* open at the *breech,* allowing the shooter to insert a shell into the end of the barrel before snapping it closed to fire. They typically have no magazine and spent casings must be removed manually. *Break-action* shotguns are commonly used for hunting and are carried broken open inside a crooked arm to prevent accidental discharges. Double-barrelled shot-guns tend to be break-actions, with the barrels either side by side or over and under; the shooter has the option of firing either barrel or both at the same time.

The famous Winchester M1887 shotgun successfully introduced *lever-action.* This early *repeater* mechanism had a lever beneath the trigger guard that could be dropped down and then raised back up with a metallic double click, ejecting a spent shell casing and loading a fresh one from a tubular magazine beneath the barrel into the firing chamber. But at the time, shells were generally made of waxed cardboard and the lever mechanism could crack open the casing or damage the shotgun itself, besides making it more difficult to fire from a prone position.

Figure 20 Double-barrel shotgun, opened to show break-action.

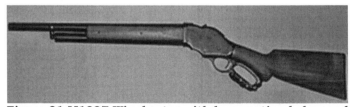

Figure 21 M1887 Winchester with lever-action below and behind the trigger guard.

The next development was the *pump-action* shotgun, which incorporates a slide built into the tubular magazine. The slide is typically pulled toward the shooter and then pushed back into position, causing the classic *ratcheting* shotgun sound, ejecting the expended shell casing, and loading the next one into the firing chamber from the tubular magazine. A subset of pump-action shotguns are *riot guns,* with shorter barrels for close-range maneuverability. Riot guns are popular with police and military, as well as homeowners with attitude.

Figure 22 Armed Response Team member cradling a Mossberg 500, hand on the pump.

Finally, some modern and usually expensive shotguns are semi-automatic. When a shot is fired, the shotgun ejects the casing and loads another round into the firing chamber from the tubular magazine beneath the barrel or from a detachable box magazine, just like a semi-auto handgun or rifle. Note that pump-action shotguns, in the hands of an experienced shooter, aren't much slower than semi-auto ones.

Most shotguns are *smoothbore,* because there's no point in imparting a spin to the dozens or hundreds of small metal balls that are jostling randomly as they accelerate down the barrel. As well, the mass of pellets does not interact in a meaningful way with any rifling a shotgun may possess, meaning there are no striations imparted to a shotgun pellet. Unless the pellets recovered from a shotgun crime scene can be traced to a specific manufacturer, through either a *mold marking* or the pellets' metallic composition, they generally cannot be traced back to an individual weapon and therefore have little evidentiary value.

Shotguns that are rifled are designed to fire a shotgun *slug*, with a single projectile, as well as pelleted shells.

Figure 23 Shotgun slug with transparent casing, showing layers of wadding and powder, and the single, rifled slug.

Note that even with rifling present, only certain types of shotgun slugs will retain any striations; most will not. To make this even more complicated, sometimes the rifling is on the slug or slug casing, called a *sabot*, creating a projectile that can be fired from any shotgun with reasonable accuracy and at longer distances than pelleted shells.

All of this elevates the shell casing to the starring role in forensic shotgun ballistics. A shotgun utilizes the same firing mechanism components as a rifle, including firing pin, breech block, ejector, and extractor, and each of these can leave markings on the plastic casing's brass base. Sometimes these will be sufficient to finger a specific shotgun; sometimes it can only point to a certain brand or type of shotgun; and sometimes, if the brass degrades in the firing, it's useless. If a shotgun murderer picks up the bits of shell casing, especially the brass base, and removes them from the crime scene, there may be no trace evidence pointing to his weapon at all.

Ammunition

Historically, bullets were made from soft lead. It was cheap, readily available, easily mined, melted at low temperatures, easily molded into the desired shape, and packed a solid kinetic punch. The scene in Mel Gibson's movie *The Patriot*, melting lead soldiers over a campfire to form bullets, is historically accurate. Soldiers without a campfire, for whatever reason, could be in serious difficulty if they ran into the enemy the day after a battle (when they'd be low on ammo). Even when the integrated cartridge was invented in 1845, replacing most homemade ammunition, they still used black gunpowder and soft lead bullets.

Until 1884. That's when Paul Vielle invented *smokeless powder* and turned firearms and ammunition manufacturing on its head. The soft lead bullets tended to melt into a too-liquid state when subjected to smokeless powder's higher explosive charge, and when they engaged the rifling, bullets generally left a layer of themselves behind in the gunbarrel. It didn't take long to render the gun useless through this *fouling.* Alloying the lead with antimony or tin, or coddling the bullet's base in a copper cup, helped a little but not a lot, especially as shooters continued pushing for an ever-longer field of fire.

Two years later, the French came out with the *Lebel rifle,* the world's first modern infantry rifle, and powering it was a *jacketed* bullet. This had a lead core but an outer layer of something tougher, such as steel, copper alloys, cupronickel, or gilding metal (a sort of brass). The harder metal prevented the soft lead from melting too much, protected the gunbarrel against fouling, and incidentally doubled the effective range of the previously used black powder rifles.

Variations on the jacketed bullet remain the most commonly fired ammunition today:

◆ A *full-metal jacketed* bullet extends the harder metal over all of the lead core, with the exception of the bullet's base. This type of ammunition can actually be too solid to inflict serious injuries, because it can pass straight through both hard and soft targets without causing a lot of damage en route.

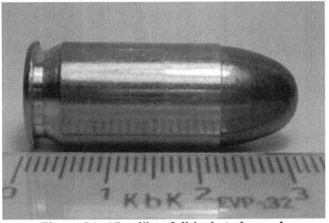

Figure 24 .45 caliber full-jacketed round, 32mm in total length.

♦ A *soft-point* bullet or *dum-dum* doesn't extend the hard jacketing all the way, leaving the bullet's tip uncoated. This ammo causes more serious injuries, because the exposed lead expands when it hits the target, forcing the hard metal jacket to expand, as well, and spreading the injury over a larger area (e.g., punching a bigger hole in the victim).

♦ A *hollow-point* bullet leaves the tip exposed and, instead of rounding out to a point or cone, or forming a flat surface, the bullet's nose is indented or hollowed out into a small cavity. This increases the amount of exposed lead, which in turn increases the rate at which the lead expands, forcing the hard metal jacket to expand more quickly, as well, and increasing the damage even further.

Note that as a bullet expands, its velocity diminishes and its punching power is reduced, meaning that it won't travel as far into the target. As a rule of thumb when comparing bullets of the same caliber, the harder the nose, the deeper and smaller the wound; the softer the nose, the more shallow and brutal the wound. Full-metal jacketed ammunition is generally preferred over longer distances and on battlefields, where expanding ammo, including soft-points and

Figure 25 9mm hollow-point round.

hollow-points, has been prohibited by the Hague Convention of 1899. (The Convention also banned exploding projectiles for hand-held firearms and bullets designed to ensure an injured soldier dies or suffers more.) Expanding ammunition is very popular among law enforcement officers, target shooters, and homeowners, not least because of its tendency to reduce so-called *collateral damage.* This means a soft-point or hollow-point is likely to remain within the intended target, rather than punch all the way through him, through the adjacent wall, and into whoever or whatever happens to be on the other side.

Of course, ammunition should fit the firearm. A famous case from 1940 involved the assassination of former British diplomat Michael O'Dwyer in London by Indian revolutionary Udham Singh. The gunman, wielding a World War I-era Smith & Wesson .455 revolver, jumped onto a public platform at Caxton Hall in Westminster and began blazing away, his gun eighteen inches from his intended victims. O'Dwyer died from his injuries after being shot twice in the back at point-blank range. But incredibly, the bullets seemed to bounce off of Lawrence Dundas, Marquess of Zetland; Sir Louis Dane; and the eighty-year-old Charles Cochrane-Baillie, Baron Lamington, all former British administrators in India. Ballistics examination by the legendary expert Robert Churchill showed that Singh's ammunition was .40 caliber, sufficiently smaller than the .455 revolver's chambers so that each bullet wobbled along the barrel rather than accelerated, reducing its kinetic punch to a trickle.

As well, the cartridges contained black powder and soft lead bullets which were three decades old at least, possibly more, further reducing any punch they might have retained. The bullet that killed O'Dwyer was the only one that flew straight.

This leads to another point; ammunition should be fresh. Both black powder and smokeless powder can deteriorate over time, and it's not unknown for a defensive homeowner to fire the old revolver, kept for years beneath the bed, at an intruder, only for the equally old ammo to misfire or the small caliber bullet to bounce off the intended victim's forehead due to the gunpowder's advanced age.

Note that ejected shell casings have withstood a contained explosion and therefore are *hot*. Second-degree burns are not uncommon amongst shooters who insist upon wearing skimpy clothing while firing. Female shooters wearing open-necked blouses tend to catch shell casings somewhere personal and proceed to dance around while removing the offending brass. If left against skin for too long, a hot shell casing can fuse with the upper epidermal layers and stick there. Some weapons throw the casing a remarkably long way and three to five feet is average, so being hit with someone else's brass at an open range would be a believable way for romantically inclined shooters to meet.

Ammunition for shotguns, of course, is different. A shotgun shell typically contains pellets or shot, a bunch of little round balls packed into the plastic or cardboard casing along with the gunpowder and protecting wads. Shot comes in various sizes and is selected to fit the intended target, with smaller shot most suitable for hunting birds (*birdshot*) and mid-sized shot good for skeet or trap shooting. Larger shot is used for hunting game, including deer (*buckshot, note the pellet size in the illustration to the right*). It's also popular with the military, law enforcement, and homeowners.

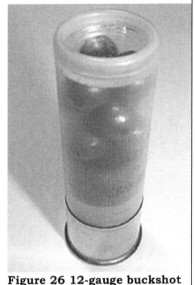

Figure 26 12-gauge buckshot in transparent casing.

Lately the trend in shotgun pellets has been away from lead, which they say can collect in water sources, and toward more inert materials, such as tungsten, bismuth, and steel. Of course, the classic lead-free alternative for self-loading shotgun owners is rock salt. It generally doesn't cause serious injury but it stings like fire in dozens or hundreds of little wounds, serving as a warning to backwoods trespassers. Commercial rock salt shells are becoming increasingly popular as riot control measures, particularly in Europe.

Selecting a firearm

Two words on caliber: size matters. Bullets from large caliber weapons punch large caliber holes; those from small caliber weapons punch small ones. While it's true that a .22 can kill just like a .45, the .45 makes it much more certain.

Figure 27 Caliber comparison. From left to right: 9mm Luger, 7.62, .357 SIG, 10mm auto, .40 S&W, .45 GAP, and .50 AE.

If, of course, the shooter can control the .45 and hit what she's aiming at. The larger the caliber, the larger the shell and the more explosive power packed in there. A .22 copper-jacketed high-power round delivers 259 joules of energy; a similar jacketed high-power .45 round gives 616 joules. This translates into what's called *recoil* or *kick,* the equal and opposite reaction to the controlled explosion. The weapon slams back and potentially throws the shooter off balance, at the same time shoving her hand, wrist, forearm, and the weapon up and toward her. A small person, without a lot of mass to ground her, firing a .45 or other large caliber pistol for the first time and without training, can literally be knocked on her ass. And of course, she'll miss. (Note that this is *not* sexist, but unfortunately true.) But if she's firing a .22, .32, or even a .38, her chances of keeping her

Figure 28 M1911, the classic military .45 caliber.

balance and hitting her target improve.

The best way to select a firearm is to try it in a gunshop, many of which have *indoor ranges* for that purpose. A beginning shooter with time to learn the basics and become accustomed to the firearm is better off starting with a smaller caliber handgun, such as the much-laughed-at .22 or a .32. Once some proficiency is gained, and once some wrist- and hand-strength have been developed, the shooter can move into higher calibers. There are also grip-strengthening devices to speed the beginner along this path.

However, if there's no time for deliberate lessons, if the shooter is in an emergency situation and grabs the closest firearm for self-defense, one hopes she's a quick learner.

Caliber is the measured diameter of the barrel. *Lands* are the raised areas, while *grooves* are the depressed areas. In the U.S., some weapons are measured from groove to groove, making the caliber seem ever-so-slightly larger. Other U.S. weapons, and just about everywhere else, the measurement is commonly from land to land, and so the weapon seems a hair smaller. As well, most nations other than the U.S. measure caliber in millimeters, and so experienced shooters tend to become adept at comparing the two in their minds. As a rather useless but interesting side note, the two measurement systems cross at the .380 Auto Colt Pistol (ACP) and 9x17mm Browning ammunition, which are the same size.

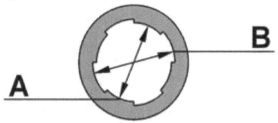

**Figure 29 How to measure a firearm's caliber:
land to land, or groove to groove.**

There's no problem translating 9mm as "nine millimeter" or even 9x17mm as "nine by seventeen millimeter," but Imperial units sometimes make readers pause, wondering how .22 cal or .303 or .455 should be properly worded. As a hint, ignore the decimal. It's "twenty-two caliber" or "two-two caliber," "three-aught-three," and "four fifty-five" or "four-five-five."

Shotguns, of course, throw all this upside down. Rather than being measured in milimeters or inches, shotguns are measured based upon the weight of a solid ball of lead that fits through the barrel. A shotgun with a barrel sized to accommodate a lead ball weighing 1/12th of a pound is called a 12 *gauge*. If it holds a larger lead ball that weighs 1/8th of a pound, it's an 8 gauge, and a smaller shotgun fitting a ball weighing 1/20th of a pound is a 20 gauge. As this shows, the larger the number, the smaller the shotgun, which tends to confuse those holding only a passing acquaintance with the beasts. However, if shooters pause to put the shotgun's gauge into the fractional format (put the one over the slash), the differences quickly become clear.

Another consideration in shotguns is *choke,* which is a slight constriction at the barrel's mouth. This forces those tumbling pellets closer together so they take longer spreading out, increasing the shotgun's effective range and its accuracy over distance. But paradoxically, an improvement in accuracy can decrease the odds of hitting the target at shorter ranges, if the shooter's aim is off. Some shotguns have screw-on barrel endings with different chokes, allowing the pellet spread to be altered for different targets (clay, partridge, turkeys, bucks, or home intruders).

For serious homeowners, there's nothing like a shotgun. At close range, it has the most effective stopping power of all, and hardened criminals wet their drawers at the sound of a pump-action's ratchet in a small, darkened room. It's an unmistakable sound and intimidating to anyone who recognizes it. Because the pellets spread out after leaving the barrel, the shooter doesn't have to aim perfectly to cause significant injuries, allowing her to engage multiple targets more easily. And since preventing injuries to family members and other innocent bystanders is a priority in such situations, a shotgun's pellets are less likely to penetrate walls, reducing the odds of collateral damage.

When the American Expeditionary Force reached France in 1917, some were armed with short-barrelled 12-gauge pump-action shotguns, bayonets attached. Called trench guns, the doughboys found them brutally effective —

so effective that the Kaiser's government filed a diplomatic protest, claiming they violated the standards of war. (This was more than two full years after the French deployed tear gas and the Germans chlorine gas, both outlawed in 1899 by the Hague Convention. So much for the standards of war.) The German protest received short shrift and in the Second World War, both Allied-supplied partisans and jungle-fighting Marines found the trench gun had retained its effectiveness.

Figure 30 One of my favorite photos from World War II. U.S. Marine fighting in the Pacific Theater, carrying a 12-gauge, pump-action Winchester M97 shotgun.

Most riot guns (as distinguished from other pump-action shotguns), now often called *tactical shotguns* by law enforcement professionals, are 12 gauge, too, and most non-lethal shells (beanbags, tear gas rounds, rubber slugs, electric shock rounds, and those designed to make loud noises to scare intruders and other animals away) are made to fit that bore. Homeowners, on the other hand, might gravitate toward 20-gauge riot guns. The riot gun's shorter barrel makes it easier to manage, especially indoors, and the lighter gauge not only inhibits the pellets from penetrating walls, it also delivers less of a kick. As well, riot guns typically have little choke, providing a lot of spread over a small bit of space.

What's involved in a ballistics examination?

When police gather evidence at a crime scene, there are three possibilities for firearms-related evidence:

1. Finding a firearm, but neither ammunition, fired bullets, or spent cartridge casings.
2. Finding some combination of the above, for example, a loaded firearm or a firearm seized from a suspect and spent cartridge casings collected at the scene.
3. Finding some combination of related evidence, such as fired bullets and cartridge casings, but no firearm.

When only a firearm is found, the ballistics examination focuses on learning that weapon's specifics, such as its make and model, caliber, whether it shares other characteristics of its class of firearm (lands and grooves, rifling twist, typical firing behavior, and so on), and how it marks both bullets and casings.

When only related evidence is found, the examiner seeks to determine if it carries any value for a possible court case by indexing the microscopic markings, for comparison to a firearm should one be located. In addition, he can find the best possible match for the make or model of weapon that fired it and the ammunition manufacturer that made it, giving investigators clues of what to search for.

When both are found, the end goal is to determine whether the firearm actually fired (or chambered, in the case of unfired or dud ammo) the recovered bullets and casings, or if it's a plant. Along the way, the examiner performs all the steps in the two analyses above.

Chain of custody, evidence collection, and sequence of examinations

When a firearm is seized at a crime scene, the investigator responsible begins what's called its *chain of custody,* the paper trail proving where the evidence was at any given time, who had control over it, who had access to it, what tests were performed on it, and how it was transferred from department to department or agency to agency. They're usually pre-printed, padded forms, filled out at the crime scene or police station, and enclosed with the firearm when it's sent to the lab.

The chain of custody documentation is designed to prevent or disprove allegations of evidence planting or tampering by investigators. For example, if the chain of custody is sound and unbroken, it can be proven that a revolver found at a murder scene is the same revolver analyzed by forensic ballistics experts and then presented in court. But if there are discrepancies in the chain of custody, the defendant can move to have the ballistic evidence thrown out.

Information written down should include the serial number, make, model, caliber, and importer, if applicable. This basic info should be marked on the pad and also on the firearm itself, usually in the lab with an engraver or permanent marker, in some inconspicuous manner that doesn't subtract from its value. The collecting officer must be sure he's got the right serial number and manufacturer; some weapons are marked with the retailer's name and others with a patent number or ammunition data.

At this early stage of the investigation, a decision must be made as to which tests should be performed first. Tests conducted upon stuff that deteriorates, such as fingerprints and blood spatter, should be conducted before the test firing and drop testing.

If the weapon is stained with blood or any other pertinent matter, it should be wrapped in clean paper that's taped in place to preserve the evidence. To preserve fingerprints and prevent adding new ones, the firearm should be handled as little as possible. Although wearing gloves helps, they can smudge latent prints, and so even then the collecting officer should only touch the firearm in an area unlikely to contain prints or where it's impossible to lift them, such as the rough part of the slide on a semi-auto. The grip on the Beretta below shows rough areas where fingerprints wouldn't stick.

Figure 31 Beretta 8045 with textured grip, which wouldn't be useful for normal fingerprinting.

When fingerprints are suspected, the firearm should be tied with string onto a wooden plank or cardboard sheet, to ensure it doesn't shift about and make contact with other objects; pegboard works pretty well.

All firearms should be packed and transported in strong cardboard or wooden boxes. They shouldn't be cleaned, either inside the breech, inside the barrel, or outside, prior to being examined. If it's a semi-auto, the magazine should be removed; both semi-autos and revolvers should have any rounds removed from the breech. A loaded firearm in a ballistics laboratory is a disaster waiting to happen.

Initial firearm examinations

When a forensic ballistics specialist (also known as a firearm examiner) begins analyzing a weapon that's just arrived in the lab, some specific steps are followed:

1. Double-check the firearm is unloaded. This is a mandatory first step in any examination.
2. Confirm the make, model, and serial number. This can be trickier than it sounds. As an example, Beretta 8000 models (the Cougar series) are manufactured in various calibers, and each has the specific caliber of required ammunition engraved on the slide, along with the serial number, but not necessarily the Beretta name. The 8040 model, therefore, could be misidentified as a .40 calibre Smith & Wesson, because .40 S&W, the appropriate ammo type, is engraved beside the serial number. The 8357 model is engraved .357 SIG, and the 8045 as .45 ACP.
3. Confirm the weapon's calibre to ensure no changes have been made from the manufacturer's original design. This can be done by measuring the bore diameter or the breech, or taking a cast of a revolver's chamber. Online research is also appropriate, to ensure the examiner understands the firearm's design; many older rifles were manufactured for various military outfits around the world, and each has its own ammunition specifications.
4. Determine the firearm's action type (single or

double for a revolver, semi-auto or full auto).
5. Determine what type of safety is employed.
6. Make sure no other alterations have been made to the firearm.
7. Note any after-market add-on equipment (laser sights, special grips) as well as the sighting mechanism.

A separate and special examination is made of the gunbarrel:
1. Triple-check to ensure the barrel is free from projectiles.
2. Check the barrel for foreign matter (blood, other biological matter, gunshot residue). If found, the firearm will need to be examined by the appropriate lab *before* any more tests are performed.
3. Count the lands and grooves and note the twist.
4. Look to see if the barrel has been damaged in any way. This is vital before any test-firing is performed.
5. Examine the rest of the firearm for damage, especially the breech and firing mechanism.

Forensic ballistics testing

Once the firearm has returned to the ballistics lab, fingerprints and biological examinations complete, the next round of testing begins. These tests depend upon the type of firearm.

Revolvers:
1. Open or remove the cylinder.
2. Check the cylinder for damage and look for smoke haloes, little rings of residue that form around the opening of the chamber after it's been fired. This may or may not help determine which and how many chambers have seen recent action.
3. Close or replace the cylinder and check the cylinder stop by cocking the hammer and trying

to turn the cylinder. The stop should prevent it from moving. This step should be performed for all chambers. For double-action revolvers, the hammer must be held back manually.

4. Check the safety system employed to ensure it's working properly.

Semi-auto handguns:

1. Check the magazine's capacity by loading it with dummy rounds of the appropriate caliber until no more will fit. Insert the loaded mag into the pistol and ensure it will engage and function normally, then remove it, remove the dummy rounds from the mag, and count them.
2. Pull back the slide and engage the slide lock, if there is one, or hold it back manually while examining the extractor and ejector mechanisms.
3. Check to see if it's actually a fully automatic beast (machine gun) disguised as a semi-auto. Sometimes a pistol has been altered by a gunsmith, amateur or professional, and these "custom" firearms don't always have any external indicator, such as a *rate-of-fire selection switch,* to show that it's now capable of rapid fire. If a selector switch is present, fire a minimum of three rounds on full auto-fire mode at the lab's indoor range using a *remote firing device,* squeezing and holding the trigger in one remote pull and confirming the firearm's status as fully automatic by design.

   If there's no selection switch, the examination is a bit more detailed. Cock the hammer, then squeeze the trigger and hold it while dragging the slide to the rear and releasing it. Then release the trigger and squeeze it again. If the firing mechanism releases or "goes off," then it's an ordinary semi-auto. If there's no release, it's been customized and it's capable of fully automatic fire by

49

modification. Again, the examiner should take the pistol to the lab's indoor range and fire a minimum of three rounds on full auto, with one trigger pull, to confirm this.

4. Check the safety systems to ensure they're working properly, both active (safety catch) and passive (an internal gizmo called a *disconnector bar* that prevents the trigger from connecting with the firing mechanism).

Shoulder-fired long guns, whether rifle or shotgun:

1. If there's a magazine, check its capacity as described in the first step for semi-auto pistols.
2. Ratchet a round into the chamber to ensure the loading system is working properly.
3. Check to see if the weapon is fully automatic, as described in the third step for semi-auto pistols, except instead of dragging back the slide, the examiner should cycle the action in its appropriate manner.
4. If this is a shotgun, measure the choke if applicable. This can be done by checking the markings on the barrel, or measuring the muzzle's interior diameter and comparing it to the barrel's mouth.
5. Finally, test the safety mechanisms, similar to the fourth step in the semi-auto section above.

When testing safety systems on any firearm, if the first test fails, that might mean the safety failed or it might mean the test was performed incorrectly. A second or even third test is generally required by lab protocols.

Now that the examiner is thoroughly familiar with the firearm in question, it's time to move on to more specific analyses. For all firearms, regardless of variety or its involvement in a crime, there are a number of basic tests to be performed. Many of these tests require the weapon be placed within a *machine rest,* a sort of mobile rack on wheels, not much larger than the actual weapon and designed to be set on a table or other flat surface, both within the lab and on the range. Some machine rests have longer or telescoping legs, enabling them to work without the table. The machine rest removes the human element from the testing procedures and ensures greater accuracy.

Trigger weight test:

How much strength does it take to pull a particular firearm's trigger? If a disgruntled new widow claims the semi-auto kept beneath her husband's pillow had a hair-trigger and she brushed against it in the night, accidentally blowing out his brains, this test assumes greater importance.

There are three different instruments that measure trigger pull: *digital scales, spring scales,* and *trigger weights.* Which an examiner uses depends upon which is available within her lab, or which is designated as standard procedure within his department.

Spring scales have a narrow tube with a fixed needle and shifting weight measurements along a gauge window. Attached is a spring-loaded rod with a hook on the end. They've been around since at least 1941, but early models weren't all that accurate and they didn't spread far within accuracy-conscious labs. Digital scales have a digital readout within a hand-held gauge, with the same spring-loaded, hooked rod attached. They're of course much more modern. Both types of scales require maintenance or they'll lose accuracy over time, which might have been part of the problem in the 1940s.

They also both operate in a similar manner. Fasten one end of the spring scale to a fixed surface (and it would likely be stored that way in the lab, perhaps permanently attached). Cock the firearm being tested, place the hook on the trigger, and slowly pull the weapon away until it fires. (Of course it wouldn't be loaded for the test; the examiner would

J. Gunnar Grey

hear the clack of the firing mechanism and the hammer would snap forward. Also, the weapon could be within a machine rest on a flat surface, and the examiner would move the rest, not the firearm itself.) An experienced examiner would be watching the readout and see the exact amount of weight that fired the gun.

With a digital scale, there's no need to fix one end in place (and so it would more likely be put away within a drawer or cabinet between uses). With the firearm handheld or locked within a machine rest, place the hook around the trigger and pull until it discharges, watching the weight required.

Trigger weights are different. They're an older system and so more likely to be still in use within labs suffering under limited budgets. They also require more time to perform the test, setting up arguments between lab workers and supervisors over which costs more, the new piece of equipment or the firearm examiner's time.

The usual hooked rod this time is rather longer, more than a foot long, and it's designed to sit upright independently on a flat surface. There's an assortment of round, flat metal weights in various sizes, usually ¼, ½, 1, 2, and 5 pounds. The examiner places weights on the rod, puts the hook above the trigger, and lifts the firearm straight up (meaning there's no machine rest used in this test). If the weights come off the table before the firearm discharges, the examiner must add more weight and repeat the test. If the firearm discharges first, then the examiner will take off some weight and try again. The object is to find the least amount of weight that will fire the weapon before the weights leave the table.

Note that single-action weapons must be cocked between trigger-weight testing attempts, while double-action, semi-auto, and full auto firearms would not need this. Every chamber of a revolver must be tested separately and differences noted. The typical trigger pull for a home-defense firearm should be above 4.5 pounds, to help prevent accidental discharges. For hunting weapons in rugged field conditions, it should stay above 3.5 pounds, while varmint or plinking weapons can go to 2.5. Note that the latter, or anything lighter, qualifies as a hair-trigger. For sport target shooting, check the regulations; some of these go into ounces rather than pounds. On the other end of the scale, pun intended, military trigger pull is generally between 6 and 8 pounds. An experienced firearms examiner can guesstimate trigger pull before performing the test, reducing the time required with trigger weights.

Home-made trigger-weight systems can be constructed from an S-shaped metal rod or cut-out with a pan of some sort dangling from the bottom end. Place items of known weight, such as a bag of dried beans or unopened jar of peanut butter, in the pan until the weapon fires. Or use loose sand or rocks and weigh them after the discharge, accounting for the weight of the tool, as well.

Again, of course the firearm must be unloaded, and confirmed to be unloaded, before this test is performed. But within a novel, it could be a good way to get rid of or at least scare an unpopular or dangerous examiner at a lab. The examiner's tendency would be to lean back and watch the weights on the lab table rather than lean over the weapon. With the digital and spring scales, the examiner stands to the side and watches the readouts.

Test-firing:

Each lab has a set of protocols to be followed when test-firing a weapon. There are also various *bullet recovery systems.* But the process generally follows the same pattern:

1. Lock the firearm into the *remote firing device* (machine rest with a trigger-pulling system). It's a

good idea to dry test-fire it once it's locked in, without ammunition of any sort, to ensure the firearm will function properly as arranged.

2. Some labs mark the cartridge casing and bullet prior to firing; others do it afterward. And some bullets and casings are too small to mark accurately, in which case after firing, they're stored in marked containers. Accuracy in this step is extremely important.

3. Turn on the lab's exhaust system. Firing a gun releases all sorts of chemical gasses, and while the smell may be exciting to dedicated shooters, it can also be dangerous in enclosed spaces.

4. Turn on any warning system. This may be a red light outside the range door, a warning buzzer or siren, or the examiner stating, "I'm about to fire." Most bullet recovery systems are located on the ground floor or basement of the lab building, within the indoor range, away from sensitive equipment and nerves.

5. Initial testing is usually performed with only one cartridge loaded. Some labs permit two. More would be highly unusual and most likely against laboratory protocols.

6. Align the remote firing device so the firearm's muzzle is properly aligned with the bullet recovery system.

7. Put on appropriate hearing and eye protection. Some labs insist on bullet-proof clothing, as well.

8. Activate the remote firing device with the examiner a safe distance from the weapon. Guns have been known to explode or come apart during firing.

9. Retrieve the fired bullet.

When test-firing, step-by-step notes must be kept. Weapons with more than one firing mode (single- or double-action, semi-auto or fully automatic) must be tested in all possible modes and strict notes kept (in full-auto fire, which bullet fired first, which second, and so on). The ballistics for each can vary, and the best possible testing is useless if the examiner forgets which bullet was fired in which mode.

A thoroughly modern bullet recovery system can look remarkably space age, especially stainless steel *water recovery tanks,* but old-fashioned *cotton boxes* that look primitive by comparison work just as well. The purpose of the system is to decelerate and stop the bullet within a short space and then capture it, without marring the microscopic detail on its surface. Of course, it's nice if this can be accomplished without injuring the examiner, as well.

Early bullet recovery systems, dating back to the first days of test-firing, use a box, roughly 10 x 1.5 x 1.5 feet, built of heavy plywood or metal plates. The top is hinged, allowing it to be packed with cotton, and one end has a *firing port,* with a circle cut out and a metal ring to help position the firearm's muzzle. There may be a boilerplate backstop with sand packed in front of it, to discourage high-velocity or fully jacketed rounds from slamming through the box's far end. Typically the cotton in the front of the box is moistened, to prevent *muzzle flash* from setting it on fire. (Note: this doesn't always work.) Such boxes are easily to build and the lab's maintenance department can always throw together a new one if needed.

It can take a long time to dig the bullet out of the cotton, and each bullet must be removed before another one can be fired. (And then the box must be repacked.) To help this, examiners place cardboard sheets vertically within the cotton every foot or so; he can lift out the sheets one by one until he finds the one that hasn't got a bullet hole in it, and narrow down the search to that area. As well, since there's always the possibility the examiner's aim might be off, the bullet could slam through the box's side, whether wooden or metal.

Water recovery tanks can also be made locally, but they require welding and so are more often purchased, making them a bigger outlay for the budget. (They became commercially available in the 1980s.) This is a stainless steel box, ten feet long, five feet high, and two feet wide, filled with water to just below the level of the firing port, which is sct on one narrow vertical side near the box's top, angling down at 30°. That's a solid and heavy piece of equipment, and if the lab has one, again, it's most likely to be located on the ground floor or in the basement.

The bullet enters the water at a 30° angle, minimizing damage to the bullet and preventing most riccochets off the water's surface. It travels down through the water to the bottom corner of the box, slowing and stopping over that roughly twelve-foot distance and settling to the bottom, where a basket is waiting to catch it for retrieval. The water tank's top generally has an assisted means of lifting its hinged, heavy, air-tight, and sealed lid, and the basket is then raised with the test-fired bullet inside. There's a drain in one corner so lead- and chemical-contaminated water can be removed, the interior is a light color with underwater lighting, and the best are equipped with a nonskid firing platform with work area.

When test-firing, all the usual protective gear applies, including an exhaust system.

Drop and shock testing:

Sometimes a person is shot and it's claimed the firearm was dropped and went off accidentally. In these cases, drop testing and shock testing must be performed to ascertain the likelihood of that event. Because these tests can damage the firearm, they'll usually be the last tests performed by the lab.

For *drop testing,* an inch-thick rubber mat is placed atop a good, solid floor, typically concrete or cement. Load the firearm with a *primed cartridge casing* (basically a blank with only primer, not gunpowder); if it's a revolver, be sure it's loaded into the firing chamber. Cock the hammer, disengage the safety, and drop the weapon onto the mat from waist height (three feet or so). Then pick it up and check the cartridge casing for firing pin impact markings (rimfire or centerfire). If it's marked, then the weapon will fire when dropped; if there's no marking, it won't.

Drop testing should be performed on every possible side, including the weapon's top, bottom, muzzle, hammer, right side, and left side, and it should be performed with any safety catch both engaged and disengaged. For revolvers, examiners should test every chamber.

Shock testing is similar, but instead of dropping the firearm, it's locked into a machine rest and struck with a bit of lab equipment called a *dead blow hammer.* This is a type of mallet that's designed to minimize both hammer rebound and damage to the item being struck. They come in different sizes, weights, and varieties, but typically they're orange or black and made of polyurethane, sometimes with fiberglass or rubber-covered handles. The dead blow hammer's head is hollow and generally filled with sand or lead shot, which can leak out on impact. There's a possibility of trace evidence corruption, which is another reason shock testing is one of the very last lab tests performed.

Again, every chamber must be tested for revolvers, and double-action weapons must be tested in every possible mode. The firearm must be struck from every possible angle, and with any safety catch engaged and disengaged.

"Accidentally" loading a firearm prior to this test could kill the examiner or cause some real property damage, while loading a blank rather than a primed cartridge casing would scare the pants off them. While that would be an acceptable plot device in fiction, such behavior if traced to the perpetrator would likely lead to loss of license in real life, at the very least.

Bullet examinations

In a perfect investigation, the bullets recovered from a crime scene or from a victim's body will be well formed despite the battering it received, still in one piece, and carry sufficient rifling marks to find the precise gun that fired it. The comparison of a fired and unfired bullet, below, shows near perfection. But most cases aren't perfect.

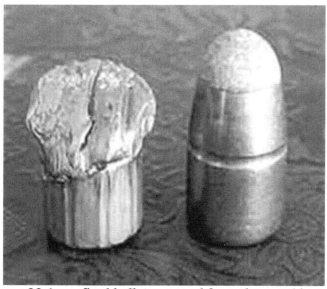

Figure 32 An unfired bullet removed from the cartridge and a fired bullet, showing the damage that can ensue as well as excellent rifling striations on the bearing surface with a right-hand twist.

A perfect lab report on a perfect recovered bullet would include:
1. All descriptive information, such as caliber, manufacturer, and ammunition type. In a slightly less than perfect report, the last two would be lists of possibilities, not exact matches.
2. The firing weapon's rifling characteristics, including the number of lands and grooves, the width

thereof, and the twist rate and direction.

3. The make and model of the firing weapon. Again, if the case is slightly less perfect, this would be a list of possibilities.
4. A determination whether the identifications made would stand up in court, meaning how valuable is this evidence.

But lab analyses and reports are perfect no more often than investigations. Bullets recovered are likely to have been squashed, warped, or shattered against hard objects such as bone or a brick wall. They might be unrecognizable, just a twisted bit of metal, and not all of the various bits might have been found so it can't even be properly judged by weight.

Figure 33 These shattered bits and pieces of metal are more common than the clear striations of the preceding photo.

If the murder weapon was a shotgun, the situation is even worse. Pellets, wadding, and many used shotgun cases can't be individuated to a weapon at all (although the metal base of the case might be). Those bits and pieces can only point toward a possible manufacturer or type of shotgun shell, although if it can be proven the suspect owned that brand, there's still some evidentiary value.

Initial examinations:

In a similar manner to firearms, the collecting officer at the crime scene will open the chain of custody. The recovered bullets, whole or shattered, must be individually packaged and labeled. If there's any sign of trace evidence, the bullets should be routed to the appropriate labs before the ballistics analysis.

The first part of the analysis covers the bullet's physical characteristics:

1. Weigh recovered bullets or parts thereof individually. This is measured in *grains* using a balance, with 437.5 grains to the ounce. Different calibers weigh different amounts but many of them overlap, so while this can help narrow things down, it won't give an exact match. Note that bullets should be carefully cleaned prior to weighing, taking extreme care not to alter the microscopic markings. Some labs use ultrasonic cleaners but these can damage evidence, so mild soap is generally preferred even though it's labor intensive.

2. Using *calipers,* preferably calipers with plastic jaws that won't scratch, measure the bullet from groove to opposite groove to find the caliber. Because the bullet's base is usually its least damaged part, that's where most measurements are taken. But if the bullet has a boat-tail and narrows at the base, it should be measured at another location on the longish, straight tubular part, called the *bearing surface.* Damaged bullets may be impossible to accurately measure. And again, there's overlap between ammo types, so at best this is only a guideline.

3. Determine the bullet's composition to help narrow down the manufacturer. Most are lead, but newer metals can include tungsten and steel. Jackets might be made from copper alloys, brass, steel, or nickel. As well, some professional or experienced shooters prefer *coated* bullets, which can increase the shooting time before a weapon needs cleaning and keep the barrel cooler (*moly*

coating or Lubalox®) although they tend to reduce the bullet's explosive power. Purchased ammo can be moly coated at home without expensive equipment; it doesn't have to be purchased that way.

A popular line of .38 Special ammo is coated with nylon for more even expansion (Nyclad®). KTW, a brand of ammo manufactured from the 1960s to the 1990s, had a steel core jacketed with hardened brass and a tip coated with Teflon®, which made riccochets from solid surfaces, such as windows, less likely. The incredibly solid bullet had little trouble penetrating Kevlar® and other protective clothing, earning it the sobriquet "cop killer bullets," but urban legend awarded the distinction to the Teflon® tip and ignored the bullet itself.

4. Determine the bullet's jacketing: full-metal (usually military), soft- or hollow-point.

5. Although firing lengthens a bullet as well as possibly deforming it, measure the slug's length, as well.

6. Some unusual rounds might have equally unusual coloring. Armor-piercing military rounds, for example, usually have an antique gold bullet and a darker tip. A light blue tip indicates an incendiary round, designed to start a fire on impact, while tracers have red or orange tips.

7. Finally, what's left of the bullet's shape can help indicate its manufacturer, as well. Whether the jacketing extends to cover the base fully, in part, or not at all; whether the base is enclosed by a copper cup; whether the base is flat, concave, conically concave, convex, or boat-tailed; whether the nose is hollow-pointed, soft-pointed, rounded, or with a long, sharp tip; all can help.

Criminals often load their firearms with rounds from different manufacturers (Winchester, Peters, Remington, Federal, Smith & Wesson, etc.) at the same time, making this process even more difficult.

The analyst takes the collected information and sorts it through the ammo specifications maintained by the Sporting Arms and Ammunition Manufacturers' Institute, Inc. (SAAMI), looking for a match. Many labs also keep collections of known ammunition with databases of manufacturers' characteristics, so analysts can check each type visually. These collections, however, aren't always the best and won't generally include new brands and types unless the lab is proactive and well-funded.

This search may not produce an exact match for the ammunition. But it can narrow down the choices facing investigators to a few limited possibilities, allowing them to purchase some boxes for test-firing and making comparisons.

General rifling characteristics:

The bullet's *class characteristics,* discussed in the last section, help indicate its design and manufacture; the *general rifling marks* made by the firearm on the bullet do the same for the weapon. This analysis includes determining rifling twist direction, measuring and counting lands and grooves, and examining various microscopic markings.

A left-hand twist creates striations on the bullet that lean to the left; a right-hand twist will lean to the right, as shown below. This is easily visible with the naked eye.

The lands are the raised areas in a gunbarrel, while the grooves are the depressed areas. These create negative or inverse marks on fired bullets, like a casting, meaning the land impressions will be depressed and the groove impressions will be raised. These impressions are also easily seen and counted, but measuring them precisely calls for a comparison or stereoscopic microscope and micrometer or calipers in a technique called the *air gap method.*

Here's how it's done with a *comparison micro-scope*:

1. Place the bullet to be measured beneath one lens of the microscope.
2. Place the micrometer or calipers beneath the other with jaws open.
3. Make sure both sides have the same magnification level and focus both lenses. The side showing the bullet should have both ends of the *measurement gap* in sharp focus, although the rounded bit between them can be fuzzy.

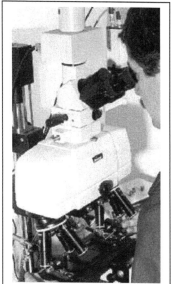

Figure 34 Comparison microscope in FBI service.

4. Adjust the microscope so that the measuring tool butts up against or overlays the bullet.
5. Open the tool's jaws the proper amount and record the measurement to the nearest one-thousandth of an inch. Then rotate the bullet to the next land or groove to be measured and repeat.

The technique is similar with a *stereoscopic microscope,* except there's only one viewing area and one lens to focus during the measuring process.

Each land and groove on a recovered bullet should be measured as precisely as possible, because manufacturer's data on barrel rifling is the quickest way to determine make and model for the weapon that fired the bullet in question. If the bullet is squished or otherwise deformed, precise measurements may not be possible, but sometimes the lands and grooves can still be counted, which in itself will narrow the field of possible weapons. If even that's not possible, sometimes it's possible to guesstimate the number of lands and grooves from the width of a surviving one and the bullet's approximate caliber.

Microscopic markings:

In addition to rifling information, a firearm (mostly revolvers) can mark a bullet in other manners that aid the ballistic specialist. These include:

1. *Shaving,* which happens when the cylinder or chamber of a revolver doesn't quite align properly and a portion of the bullet gets sliced away, leaving no rifling marks in that spot.

2. *Skid marks* or *slippage,* a sort of widening of the top edges of the rifling striations that happens between the millisecond when the bullet hits the rifling and the following millisecond, when the bullet engages the rifling. The semi-liquid bullet wobbles for a bit, forming tracks in the rifling that look remarkably like the skid marks from a car. This tends to happen more with revolvers than other firearms.

Once the analyst has all the data possible, it's time to see how close a determination of the weapon involved can be made. The FBI maintains an online database of general rifling characteristics for various weapons. The analyst can input caliber, number of lands and grooves, their measurements, the directional twist, and any other information available, and receive a list of weapons which might have fired the bullet. The list can then be narrowed down as additional information is received during the investigation.

Challenges:

Besides the very common problem of damaged, fragmented bullets that don't present sufficient data to make a feasible match, there are other problems that can crop up during a bullet examination, including:

1. There are *adapters* commercially available that fit

inside a gunbarrel like an arm inside a sleeve, so the weapon can fire a smaller caliber of ammo than it would normally take. Some of these *subcaliber inserts* are rifled, and some are not. If it is, then the recovered bullets will carry the rifling of the adapter, not the weapon. If it's not, the bullet will have no rifling marks at all.

2. Using *smaller caliber ammo* without an adapter might also leave no rifling marks on the bullet. Of course, the bullet may not pack much punch, either.

3. *Polygonal rifling,* a technique used by manufacturers including Glock, Kahr Arms, Magnum Research, and Heckler & Koch, doesn't leave rifling marks with nice, neat lands and grooves. Instead, they have rounded sides and are almost impossible to measure precisely.

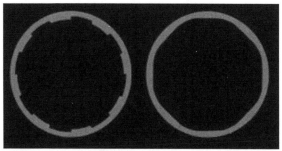

Figure 35 Common rifling pattern on the right, polygonal rifling on the left. It's much harder to measure.

4. A *coating* can inhibit rifling on a bullet. Nyclad® bullets will generally have some rifling striations, but they tend to be lighter, shallower, and in general harder to work with. Bullets with Teflon® coating tend to take almost no striation markings.

5. *Frangible* bullets, which are designed to shatter upon striking a hard surface to prevent ricochets, and *exploding* bullets, which are exactly

what they sound like, don't leave a lot behind for forensic examination. Exploding bullets were outlawed by the 1899 Hague Convention for battlefields, but while city streets are another type of battlefield, they don't always obey the rules of war.

6. *Reloaded* ammunition will typically have marks from the process. Once the firearms examiner learns to recognize these markings, they tend to be easier to sort out than some of these other challenges.

7. *Microscopic amounts* of lead and other metals are often left behind in the gunbarrel after the bullet passes through, and over time these can accumulate enough to interfere with rifling marks. Rusted or corroded gunbarrels carry the same problem.

Figure 36
Expanding ammunition, designed to mushroom open like a flower.
Note the rifling striations on the bearing surface, clearly visible.

8. *Expanding* or *mushrooming* ammunition is designed to open like a flower when it strikes its target, significantly increasing the size of the wound and just as significantly decreasing the bullet's velocity, reducing the odds of the slug passing straight through and striking someone or

something on the target's other side. Problem is, the bullet rolls back on itself, hiding any rifling marks inside. It's not possible to forensically examine the striations without fundamentally changing the bullet, and often the very act of unrolling the bullet ruins or distorts the striations.

9. Finally, if the bullet is removed from a lucky survivor, the surgeon may have gripped it with *forceps* in the process, damaging the striations.

Comparison analyses:

Of course, the preceding examinations just gather data. They don't compare that data to test-fired slugs and not many conclusions can be drawn, certainly nothing sufficient to solve a crime nor convict a criminal. To dig deeper, the firearms examiner must turn to the stereoscopic and comparison microscopes.

When examining test-fired rounds from a seized weapon, either to other test-fired rounds or to evidence bullets, there are certain steps the forensic ballistics expert follows:

1. Examine the test-fired and evidence bullets individually beneath the stereoscopic microscope and check if the firearm leaves good, strong, identifiable markings.
2. With these marks in mind, the examiner next places the test-fired or known quantity bullet beneath the right lens of the comparison microscope. The bullet's nose is generally attached to the mount.
3. Adjust the microscope's little spotlight so it hits the bullet on the long, tubular bearing surface (body) at an oblique angle. This usually shows the markings best.
4. Examine the bullet, rotating it as necessary on its long axis, to find the clearest, richest source of markings. When this is found, fasten the bullet

down in that alignment.

5. Place the evidence bullet or less-clear test-fired bullet beneath the left lens and adjust the lighting and magnification to the same direction and level as the comparison bullet.

6. Rotate the left-side bullet and look for correspondence between the two sets of striations. Check the bullet's entire surface and use higher magnification on both sides as necessary.

7. If a match is found, rotate both bullets together and see the depth of that match. It should extend (to some extent) all the way around both bullets, land by land and groove by groove, although if the evidence bullet is deformed this may not happen. The closest matching areas should be marked with a permanent marker.

8. If no match can be made to an evidence bullet, more test-firing can be done and more test-fired rounds compared. If the match still can't be made, then either the firearm in question doesn't deliver consistent rifling striations, or it's not the weapon sought in the investigation.

If a firearm was seized without related ammunition or fired bullets, the examiner compares the clearest test-fired bullet to the others, learning the markings produced by the weapon and their consistency. If evidence bullets are delivered later in the investigation, there's an existing standard for comparison.

If fired bullets or unfired ammunition (duds or misfires) are recovered without a weapon, the analyst compares them to each other to determine if they were all fired by the same firearm. If not, she tries to categorize them and figure out how many guns were fired during the crime, or perhaps if they relate back to previous crimes. The latter might be done through the FBI's or ATF's databases, through an image database or computerized search system maintained by the department or lab performing the analysis, or by manually sorting through cold case files not yet computerized. Obviously the latter requires a ton of time and only the most dedicated crime-solvers will spend possibly unpaid time digging through the old files.

If both firearms and related bullets and ammo are recovered together, the analysis combines features of both. The analyst must first compare the test-fired bullets to each other and check the markings for quality and consistency. Then he would compare the evidence slugs to each other to determine the number of weapons fired during the crime. Only then would he compare the test-fired rounds to the evidence bullets and seek a match.

Each analysis has one of three possible conclusions:

1. *Elimination,* meaning the two bullets' striations are so different they couldn't have been fired by the same weapon. This conclusion is a difficult one to reach, especially if the evidence bullet is deformed and its striations are tough to follow. When it is reached, it ends this part of the investigation.

2. *Inconclusive,* meaning the two bullets might have been fired by the same weapon, but then again, they might not. This can happen when the evidence bullet is really mangled, or the firearm has been damaged in some manner between when it fired the evidence bullets and when it fired the test bullets, or the weapon was camouflaged (perhaps with an adapter) when it fired the evidence bullets.

3. *Identification,* meaning a solid match has been made.

Figure 37 Microphotograph of a positive identification.

This works on a complicated principle called the *best known non-match*. As an example, if rounds fired from a particular 9mm Walther P38 are compared to those fired from a different 9mm Walther P38, all of the bullets will exhibit certain characteristics because they were marked by similar guns. The same thing will happen when comparing bullets fired by two .45-caliber Colt M1911s, or two .40-caliber Glock 24s, or any other two guns of the same make, model, and caliber, and manufactured by the same company during a similar time period. This is because the weapons were rifled in the same manner, with the same number of lands and grooves and with the same twist direction and degree, and perhaps even by the same machine tools. With all that similarity, the fired bullets must share some common characteristics, forensically speaking.

However, while those bullets' *class characteristics* will agree in a general sense, under the comparison microscope they'll appear vastly different. Scientific studies and computer analyses comparing thousands of firearms have repeatedly found that no two different guns, no matter how closely related, will produce more than four consecutive matching striations. A match is considered an identification if more than four such consecutive matching striations are found.

Casting:

When a law enforcement agency in another county asks to examine evidence bullets that are under active investigation and can't be spared, or when the budget or chain of custody won't permit sharing, then castings can be made and sent instead. Here's how it's done:

1. Stick a glob of mounting putty onto the end of a short wooden rod (dowels work fine) and insert the bullet's nose into the putty to hold it steady.

2. Apply a ribbon of casting material and an equal ribbon of hardener onto the coated paper provided in the casting kit, and mix them with the little wooden spatula until it begins to harden (from thirty seconds to one minute). There are several different brands to choose from and they may have differing characteristics. The material and hardener are generally two different colors so the user can judge the mixing's effectiveness, but the final result is generally a neutral tone such as black, brown, or white.

3. Scoop the mixed formula into a small (bullet-sized) container, then dip the mounted bullet into the goo to coat it. Apply several layers so it's a good, thick coat and swirl it around so all areas are covered.

4. Let it dry for the length of time stated in the instructions, typically between three to five minutes. Test it on the strip of paper; if the mixed formula has dried sufficiently to tear off the paper, then the casting should be dry, as well.

5. Remove the casting from the bullet and turn it inside out. It can now be mounted on another wooden rod for examination or shipping.

It's important to remember that the casting is the inverse or negative image of the bullet, and so it's standard procedure to compare casting to casting, never casting to bullet.

Cartridge and shell casing examinations

Often the most useful item in individuating a fired bullet to a particular firearm isn't the bullet itself, but the casing. Because they're thrown aside by the firearm during the shooting, they tend to roll into out-of-the-way and hidden places. When the criminal does a quick sweep to find and remove them, some are usually missed, and the criminal, pressed for time and increasingly anxious to leave the scene, generally either forgets how many shots were fired and so how many casings she should retrieve, or runs out of time to locate them. Besides, bullets by definition are intended to strike an object, in a murder case the victim's body, and they fragment, become distorted, and become difficult to classify. Shell casings often remain intact.

Initial examinations:

When a forensics lab receives cartridge or shotgun shell casings, a procedure similar to that for firearms is followed. A chain of custody is begun, the casing packages are marked, and basic design characteristics noted. The latter includes a description, the casing's diameter, firing pin indentations (rimfire or centerfire), and any manufacturer's markings such as logo, item number, or caliber specifications. As well, an examination should be made for trace evidence. If blood, gore, hair, paint, masonry, or other trace matter is seen, or if fingerprints are suspected, the casings should be routed to the appropriate lab prior to ballistics testing.

Tool marks examinations:

When a gun fires a bullet, two types of marks can be made on both the bullet and the casing. There are *striations,* formed when a harder object (called the tool and typically a part of the gun such as the firing pin) slams into a softer object (the casing or bullet) while one or both are in motion. A simpler word for the same marking would be scratches or grazes. Striations are by far the most common markings found on bullets, but they can be on casings, as well.

The other type of marking, *impressions,* are formed when neither is in motion but a lot of pressure is applied, or the tool is in motion striking a stationary softer object. It's most commonly an indentation of some sort. Both types of marking can carry evidentiary value.

Toolmarks that can be found on a casing include:

1. *Firing pin impressions,* either rimfire or centerfire.

Figure 39 Centerfire firing pin impression on spent shell casing.

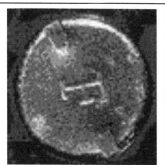

Figure 38 Rimfire firing pin impression.

2. *Firing pin drag marks,* striations engraved into the casing by the firing pin when the extractor or ejector doesn't wait for the firing pin to retract prior to grabbing the casing and throwing it out.

3. *Breech face marks,* an inverse or negative impression caused when

Figure 40 Positive identification on breech face marks.

the gunpowder explodes, the bullet flies through and out the barrel, and the cartridge casing suffers the equal and opposite reaction, slamming backward against the gun's breech face, which is the part of the firing chamber that holds the cartridge in place. The brass is hot and slightly soft, and any imperfections in the breech face, as well as its overall texture, will be transferred to the casing. Breech face marks are typically a pattern of parallel horizontal lines, a series of rings around the primer cap, or a general mottled or stippled pattern. Such markings are extremely valuable because one is literally a fingerprint of the gun's interior surface.

4. *Primer shearing marks,* striations caused by any rough edges around the firing pin hole. When a gun is fired, the breech is unlocked and the firing pin drives forward through a hole in the breech face. It's not unusual for the opening hole's edges to make drag marks on the primer cap.

5. *Chamber marks,* striations left by the firing chamber when the cartridge casing slams around inside it. If found, these will be on the casing's round wall.

6. *Extractor marks,* striations made by the extractor as it grabs the casing to throw it out. These are typically near or at the casing's rim.

7. *Ejector marks,* striations or impressions caused by the ejector tossing out the casing or an unfired bullet (misfire, dud, change of mind). Ejector marks can look different on a fired casing (which is hot when grabbed) and on an unfired bullet (which isn't) and thus can have strong evidentiary value.

8. *Anvil marks,* impressions dented into the forward edge of a rimfire's roll when the roll's other side is struck by the firing pin.

9. *Ejection port marks,* striation marks caused when the hot casing or unfired bullet smacks the edge

of the ejection port or opening in passing. Sometimes all the weapons of a particular make or model create the same type of mark on ejected casings. The M1911 is known for a certain type of ejection port mark.

10. *Magazine marks,* striations caused by sharp or rough edges on a magazine's lip. These are caused either when the shooter loads the round into the magazine, or when the firearm chambers the round from it. Note that magazine marks will change if the shooter has more than one magazine.

Comparison microscope procedures:

When examining a spent cartridge casing beneath a comparison microscope, the analysis follows a typical pattern:

1. The test-fired or known casing is always mounted on the right side, vertically with the base pointing up. If there's no test casing, the best evidentiary casing found at the crime scene goes there.

2. Adjust the microscope's lighting to highlight the casing's base. An oblique angle is usually best.

3. Rotate the casing so the little spotlight shines across the base and primer (rimfire or centerfire) at different angles to find the richest collection of markings.

4. The casing in question always goes on the left side. This may be another test-fired casing or one collected at the crime scene. It should be turned until it's at the same orientation as the casing on the right, and the light source should be set at the same oblique angle.

5. Very modern and expensive comparison microscopes have two viewing modes: split-screen or overlapping, both fully adjustable. Older ones and less expensive ones will only offer split-screen viewing, and the lab might then have a stereo-

scopic microscope for overlapping views.

6. Adjust both sides of the microscope, focusing and butting the two images together until the markings on both casings can be compared. First the class characteristics (those inherent in the casing's design and manufacture, such as caliber) are examined, then the markings made by the firing weapon. Specific attention should be paid to firing pin and breech face markings, but all should be checked. There must be enough, in both quality and quantity, to justify an individuation decision and hold up in court. Any definite matches should be indexed and marked with a permanent marker.

Note that the cartridge casing examination follows the same basic pattern as that for a fired bullet. The parallels should be no surprise.

When a forensic ballistics analyst is examining test-fired cartridge casings from a weapon found without related ammo, bullets, or casings, she will compare the best, clearest test-fired casing to her other test-fired casings. This shows how the recovered weapon marks a casing and if it does so consistently, so if a casing is submitted later in an investigation, she has the necessary information ready.

When the analyst is examining spent cartridge casings recovered without a firearm, he's trying to determine if they were all fired by the same weapon, how many weapons were fired at the crime scene, and possibly if the evidence recovered relates to previous crimes, as discussed under the bullet comparison examination, above.

When both casings and firearms are recovered together, the examination requires a few more steps. The analyst first compares the test-fired casings with each other to learn about the gun, how it marks its casings, and if it marks them consistently. She'll compare the evidence casings to each other to determine if they were all fired by the same weapon.

Then she'll compare the best test-fired casing with the evidence, looking for a match.

There are four conclusions the analyst can reach:

1. *Identification,* meaning the two casings definitely match.
2. *Inconclusive,* meaning not enough quality markings are available to support a definite match or definite elimination.
3. *Elimination,* meaning the two casings definitely do not match.
4. One or the other casing is *not suitable for examination.*

Examining unfired or misfired ammunition is similar to examining spent casings, except there generally aren't breech face markings since no controlled explosion took place. All other markings might be there, including firing pin marks that are shallow or poorly formed if the bullet misfired or proved itself a dud. The markings on unfired or misfired ammo can prove the round went through the chamber and action of a type of firearm, or possibly a particular one, depending upon the level of individuation achieved.

Sometimes criminals, especially nervous ones, ratchet rounds through a gun while mentally preparing themselves to commit a planned crime; law enforcement types refer to the markings on that ammo as "courage marks."

Challenges:

Certain problems can arise during the cartridge casing analysis:

1. Some firearms are designed to handle *more than one type* of ammunition. For example, a .357 Magnum revolver can fire .38 Special ammo, and the lab must determine which weapon fired the casings received.
2. There are *adapters* on the market that allow shotguns to fire rifle or handgun rounds. Other

adapters are designed like a sleeve that fastens inside the barrel, so the weapon can fire a different caliber or type of ammo. Lab mistakes could easily be made in such a situation.

3. If a casing, or several of them, recovered from a crime scene are split along the round edge, that's a sign it may have been fired from a weapon that doesn't properly use that ammo (but it fit into the gun and the criminal used it). Gasses typically escape along that split and so it could be blackened with residue. Note that *using the wrong ammo* is bloody dangerous, mate, and the barrel can explode.

4. If the shooter *reloads* his own rounds and he's used these casings before, the reloader will likely have left markings where the casing was gripped, resized, or crimped. These unusual markings can cause confusion, too.

5. It's possible to *camouflage* a gun so that it fools an examination. Changing the cylinder of a revolver changes the chamber marks left; swapping out the firing pin, extractor, or ejector with a new one makes the gun leave different markings on the casing; filing, abrading, or otherwise changing those interior parts will also change the markings. Although this might not make the individuation impossible (the original part might be found, or metal transfer might be proven between the weapon and a file found in the suspect's garage) it would make it a lot tougher.

Cases of ballistic interest

Individuating the bullet, part one (1912)

On October 9, a policeman in Eastbourne, a resort town on the English Channel near Beachy Head, was called to an upper-crust home to apprehend an intruder lurking in the night. Two shots were fired and Inspector Arthur Walls was killed. The killer left his hat behind but nothing else, presenting police with a tough challenge.

A series of informants led them to a man calling himself John Williams, ultimately identified as George Mackay, a "preacher's kid" from Scotland. While the hat fit Mackay, it was a common type and size. However, in a sting operation guided by informant Edgar Power, Mackay's girlfriend Florence Seymour unknowingly lead police to where a revolver was buried on the shingle beach. Unfortunately, the weapon was recovered in pieces: barrel, cylinder, hammer mechanism, and breech. The smaller bits, the springs and levers and firing pin and such, apparently had been disposed of more permanently; at some point in the investigation, a drain was mentioned.

A young gunsmith named Robert Churchill was handed the recovered parts and asked if this was the murder weapon. Individuating a firearm based upon ballistics had only been achieved with scientific accuracy earlier in the same year (see the timeline) and the challenge was both immense and groundbreaking, but Churchill was nothing if not ambitious. He reassembled the gun to working condition using bits from his workshop, test-fired it, and compared the bullets. According to his report, the two bullets were of

79

the same caliber and carried identical striations.

But in those early days of ballistic forensics, "identical striations" was a difficult concept to get across to a jury. Paul Jeserich, the German Sherlock Holmes, used microphotography to convict a killer in 1898; Churchill decided to try a wax casting. With help from Sergeant William McBride, who later led Scotland Yard's Photographic Department, he filled the barrel with dentist's wax and after it dried, eased the casting out. McBride photographed it. Churchill also prepared similar casts from dozens of other revolvers, and in court was able to show via photographs how the bullet matched up with Mackay's buried revolver and none other. The combination of Churchill's professional testimony, and Florence Seymour's giving away the revolver which proved to be the murder weapon, sent Mackay to the hangman.

What a difference one little tool makes (1920)

On December 23, 1919, armed robbers attempted a heist at a shoe factory in Bridgewater, Mass. Although the robbery was unsuccessful, witnesses got some good looks at the gang involved and police suspected Italian immigrant anarchists, looking for easy money to finance bombmaking. (In an attempt to "spread the storm of revolution to these shores," paraphrased from a propaganda flyer, anarchist groups went on a bombing spree in the United States between 1914 and 1932. Among other crimes: one anarchist dumped arsenic into a kettle of soup at a Chicago banquet attended by the local captains of industry. To his extreme frustration, nobody died.)

Four months later, on April 15, 1920, a gang of armed robbers outside another shoe factory in Braintree, Mass. were more determined. As assistant paymaster Frederick Parmenter and security guard Allesandro Berardelli escorted the factory's payroll, locked into two steel boxes, from the paymaster's office to the factory proper, they were gunned down in cold blood by two loiterers leaning against the fence of a neighboring plant. The first shooter, clean shaven, opened fire without warning; the second, wearing a ferocious walrus mustache, fired the fatal shot into Parmenter when he tried to run for it. The killers nabbed the payroll of $15,777 and were picked up by a stolen dark blue Buick waiting downhill, engine running and side curtains drawn.

The murders were utterly vicious. Berardelli lay on the sidewalk helpless, no longer reaching for the .38 in his hip pocket, when the last shots were fired into him, and the mustachioed killer shot Parmenter in the back. The coroner found six bullets in the murdered men and police collected four spent shell casings at the scene. All were .32 caliber. Five were fired from a Savage 1907 semi-auto (its advertising slogan was "Ten shots quick!"), easily identified by its peculiarly narrow rifling grooves with a right-hand twist. The other, Berardelli's final, fatal shot, came from a Colt 1903 Pocket Hammerless semi-auto, with wide grooves and a left-hand twist. Three different types of ammunition were identified, manufactured by Remington, Peters, and Winchester. Interestingly, the Winchester cartridges were of an older, outdated variety that hadn't been manufactured in years. As well, although no witness reported seeing either gunman take it, Berardelli's .38 H&R five-shot revolver, nickel-plated, was gone.

The stolen Buick was found abandoned two days later. Its wide-wheeled tracks, or those from a similar "ritzy car," were found two miles from there, in the garage of a house where lived known bombmaker and anarchist Mario Buda. The tracks were from his own car, Buda claimed, a 1914 (sometimes misidentified as a 1916) Overland crank-handled touring car with narrow wheels, currently in the garage for repairs. Police attempted to arrest the men who came to pick it up, Buda and three other Italian immigrants, Riccardo Orciani, Nicola Sacco, and Bartolomeo Vanzetti. The four were on high alert and scrambled rather than be arrested. Buda and Orciani escaped on a motorcycle; Orciani was later picked up but provided a sound alibi for the murders, while Buda reappeared in Naples, Italy. Sacco and Vanzetti raced aboard a streetcar but were hunted down and caught.

Sacco, who worked in a shoe factory, was clean shaven; Vanzetti, a fishmonger, sported a massive walrus mustache.

Figure 41 Sacco and Vanzetti, handcuffed together.

Both swore they didn't own any guns, although both were carrying at the time of their arrest. Vanzetti had a .38 nickel-plated H&R five-shot revolver, identical to the weapon missing from Berardelli's hip pocket. Although Vanzetti claimed to have purchased the .38, he knew little about it and described it as having six chambers, not five. Sacco carried an Italian passport, anarchist pamphlets, a .32 caliber Colt 1903 Pocket Hammerless (similar one shown below), and twenty-three rounds of ammunition, manufactured by Remington, Peters, and Winchester, the latter of the same damningly outmoded variety as the bullet that killed Berardelli.

Figure 42 Colt 1903 Pocket Hammerless (not Sacco's actual weapon).

During the trial, surrounded by the furor and fury of America's first Red scare, the fifty-plus witnesses to the shooting gave contradictory evidence. As bad for the defense, some of the witnesses who swore Vanzetti was peddling fish at the time admitted to having learned their lines beforehand. Despite attempts by the prosecution, the .38 H&R revolver could not be positively identified as Berardelli's. In the end, the trial boiled down to the ballistics: did the Pocket Hammerless fire Berardelli's fatal shot (Exhibit 18, also called Bullet III), or didn't it? Two defense experts, James Burns and Augustus Gill, swore it hadn't. Prosecution expert Captain Charles Van Amburgh of the Springfield Armory swore that it had; the other prosecution expert, Massachusetts State Police Captain William Proctor, said it might or might not have.

The jury looked dazed at the confusing testimony.

But one piece of evidence could not be rebutted: when forensic ballistics examiners, both prosecution and defense, went looking for more of the outdated Winchester ammunition for test-firing, they found it was so outdated that none was available — except for the rounds removed from Sacco's pocket. Prosecutor Frederick Katzmann, seeing this, did not hesitate to ask for the guilty verdict, and the jury delivered. The judge sentenced Sacco and Vanzetti to death.

Anarchists, Communists, and labor union representatives ignored the ballistics and claimed Sacco and Vanzetti had been convicted for their politics, not the crime, and the defense filed multiple motions for a retrial. During one of these in November 1923, a shady "expert witness" named Albert Hamilton disassembled Sacco's Pocket Hammerless, including the barrel, in front of the judge and the teams for the prosecution and defense. In the photo below, a Walther P99 has been field-stripped, or disassembled in the same manner. The tube second from the top is the barrel, which is interchangeable between modern firearms of the same make and model.

Figure 43 Field-stripped Walther P99. The interchangeable barrel is the second item from the top.

Beside those pieces, he then took apart two of his own Colts of the same make and model, demonstrating how the pieces were interchangeable, presumably attempting to convince his onlookers that someone had planted the guilty barrel into Sacco's Colt. He might have scored a point for the defense, casually sliding his two reassembled Colts into his pockets, except the judge, Webster Thayer, ordered him to instead leave all three Colts with the court.

Over a year later, in February 1925, Captain Van Amburgh rechecked Sacco's Pocket Hammerless and found a manufacturer's rust preventative, cosmoline, coating its barrel. That's an unmistakable sign of a brand-new, never-fired weapon, and at the very least this Colt had been test-fired by both the prosecution and defense. Hamilton blustered, claiming he hadn't switched the barrels, that some unnamed person within the prosecution must have done so. When confronted with the old barrel, now assembled into one of Hamilton's Colts, Hamilton claimed it was the wrong one and also a plant.

If Hamilton had admitted to making an honest mistake, the incident might have blown over. Instead, the defense's double-dealing destroyed their credibility, especially Hamilton's, and Judge Thayer threw out the retrial motions.

The Sacco and Vanzetti Defense Committee continued their smear campaign unabated and in response the Massachusetts governor, Alvan Fuller, impaneled a committee in June 1927 to review the case and determine a) if the two men had received a fair trial, and b) did the evidence justify their condemnation. The review committee asked advice from Colonel Calvin Goddard, one of the leading names in forensic ballistics and the man who catalogued ballistics data for every make and model of firearm manufactured. Armed with his new invention, the comparison microscope, Colonel Goddard test-fired Sacco's Pocket Hammerless and aligned the bullet under the twin lenses with Bullet III, the one that killed Berardelli. The match was so exact that Gill and Burns, the two defense expert witnesses, changed their minds and concluded Sacco's Colt had indeed fired the fatal bullet.

Two months later, on August 23, 1927, Sacco and Vanzetti died in the electric chair in Charlestown State Prison. Days before, a bomb exploded outside the home of one of the jury members who convicted them. Communist Party members demonstrated around the world. But no one could rebut the ballistics.

In October 1961, the ballistics tests on Sacco's Pocket Hammerless were repeated, using the more modern technology then available. In March 1983 the tests were repeated yet again. The findings remain unequivocal: Sacco's Colt fired Bullet III. No amount of blown smoke will ever change that one fact.

Individuating the bullet, part two (1925)

The case wasn't a complicated one. On December 16, a Vallejo, California road maintenance foreman named John McCarthy was shot and killed in his home. The fatal bullet was dug out of a wall, neighbors described the man who raced from the house shortly after the shot was fired, and McCarthy regained consciousness long enough to state he'd recently fired an employee named Martin Colwell, who precisely fit the witnesses' description. Colwell had a record as long as his houseboat scow, when arrested he carried a .38 revolver with one bullet missing, and three bullets were found in his coat pocket, as well as an opened ammo box with a few missing in his pantry. Not a lot of room for discussion there.

But when word reached the prosecutors that Colwell had hired a team of cutthroat attorneys, including as expert witness Chauncey McGovern, better known as a handwriting expert, they knew the trial would be anything but boring. To make their case bulletproof, therefore, the ballistics evidence was handed to Edward O. Heinrich, alternatively described as "the wizard of Berkeley" and "the Edison of crime detection." A multi-disciplined, coldly scientific genius, Heinrich entered more than a thousand witness stands, testifying on such diverse forensic fields as microscopy, blood spatter analysis, questioned documents (which earned him McGovern's unending ire), traffic accidents, toxicology, and ballistics. Although never a policeman, he served three years as Alameda's chief of police and also held a faculty position at UC-Berkeley. Many of his pioneering achievements would lead to standard police procedures.

A basic ballistics analysis proved to Heinrich that the fatal bullet had indeed been fired by Colwell's .38 and was of the same type as the ammunition found in his coat pocket and scow. But how to demonstrate that to the jury? Wax castings and microphotography had proven successful in courtrooms, but surely there was an even more convincing way. Heinrich placed the fatal and test-fired bullets beneath a stereoscopic microscope, perhaps best described as a single instrument joining two microscopes and giving the viewer a three-dimensional image. It took some work, but finally Heinrich rigged two cameras in place of the eyepieces and succeeded in snapping both shutters at the same moment, producing a crisp photo of the bullets in question as a single image, proving their relationship.

In trial, McGovern pooh-poohed Heinrich's achievement and managed to scramble the jury enough to hang them. But in the retrial, the jury foreman asked the judge if they could peer through Heinrich's stereoscopic microscope themselves. Seeing the original three-dimensional image helped, but the jury weren't satisfied. Next, they asked Heinrich if he could demonstrate in the courtroom how he took and developed the single-image photo. Heinrich brought in his gear, arranged it in the court's well, snapped the two shutters simultaneously, and retired to a nearby darkroom with the court bailiff as witness. When he returned, it was with a set of identical photos.

Martin Colwell was found guilty of murder and sentenced to life. He never received parole. Heinrich's photographic array received refinements and improvements through the years, but modern forensic ballistics labs use a remarkably similar system.

Individuating the bullet, part three (1929)

Most people associate St. Valentine's Day with Cupids, roses, and candy. For seven Chicago mobsters in 1929, it was the day they died.

Al Capone wanted control of Chicago. George "Bugs" Moran not only stood in his way, he was muscling in on Capone's dog-racing tracks, saloons, and bootlegging. In Capone's opinion, that made it war, and he intended to win it.

In the early morning hours, two mobsters dressed as Chicago policemen entered a garage at 2122 North Clark Street through the back door, carrying shotguns. They herded the seven men inside in front of a brick wall. They were joined by two men wearing suits, hats, and overcoats, typical mobster attire, and carrying submachine guns. The machine gunners opened fire with brutal efficiency, spraying the victims from side to side and back again, even after they collapsed onto the floor. Two of the victims, likely already dead, were then shotgunned in the face at point-blank range. Witnesses and crime scene photos show the victims were literally torn apart by seventy bullets and two shells.

When their magazines were empty, the machine gunners in civilian clothing gave their weapons to the pseudo police and exited the garage with their hands raised. The trick diverted attention long enough for Capone's murder squad to make their escape.

Six of the victims were members of Moran's gang and mobsters; one was a very unlucky mechanic, working on a truck. One victim, Frank Gusenberg, was incredibly still alive and taken to hospital with fourteen bullets in him. When asked by police who shot him, he insisted, repeatedly, "Nobody shot me," refusing to break the gangster's ethics code even then. Moran, ironically, wasn't there. He was late for the meeting, arrived to find the police there before him, and slipped away.

Although the public had been growing weary of the savage violence for a while (although not the bootleg liquor), the St. Valentine's Day Massacre ended the popular misconception of gangster glamour with a bang. Everyone wanted answers, and the Chicago police in particular wished to quell the strong public suspicion that they were actually involved in the massacre. Every machine gun associated with the department was handed over to Colonel Calvin Goddard of the Bureau of Forensic Ballistics, founded in New York City in 1925. Goddard had worked with Charles E. Waite, also a founder of the Bureau, in the development of the comparison microscope and helped prove its worth in the Sacco and Vanzetti ballistics review in 1927.

In a professionally managed ballistics investigation, Goddard examined every recovered bullet, spent cartridge casing, shotgun pellet, and shotgun case. He determined that one 12-gauge shotgun and two different Thompson submachine guns, one with a twenty-round box magazine and the other with a fifty-round drum, were used in the massacre. And he proved that no Chicago PD Thompson had been used in the slaughter.

On December 14, 1929, police tracked a wrecked, abandoned car to Fred "Killer" Burke. It had been involved in a hit-and-run traffic accident and

Patrolman Charles Skelly, who tried to apprehend the drunk driver, was shot and killed. When police raided Burke's home in St. Joseph, Michigan, they hit paydirt: a storage trunk holding two shotguns, two Thompsons, several pistols, boxes and boxes and boxes of ammunition, a bullet-proof vest, and over $300,000 in bonds stolen from a bank in Wisconsin. Goddard tested the Thompsons and proved that not only were they used in the St. Valentine's Day Massacre, one had also killed New York City mobster Frankie Yale on July 1, 1928, and may have been involved in the Milaflores Massacre in Detroit, Michigan on March 28, 1927.

Although the weapons were identified, the shooters were never proven. While Killer Burke at the very least had concealed the shotguns and Thompsons, it could not be proven he had used them. Instead, he was convicted of the murder of Charles Skelly and died in prison in 1940. Of the multiple suspects in the investigation, he was the only one to live that long; the others were murdered by fellow or rival mobsters by 1936. Bugs Moran died in Leavenworth prison in 1957. Al Capone served time for federal tax evasion and died in his home in Palm Island, Florida in 1947 after suffering a stroke, pneumonia, and cardiac arrest. He also suffered neurosyphilis; at the time of his death his doctor estimated he had the mental capacities of a twelve-year-old, spending his time raving about Communists and Bugs Moran.

Backspatter (1976)

It's possible to prove a murder case and obtain a conviction without a body when there's strong circumstantial evidence. A little-known element in ballistic forensics helped in this investigation.

A red stain on a bus barn wall, some coagulated

brown liquid in the gravel, a dental bridge, and some yanked-out hair looked ominous when Vicki Brown vanished on February 10, 1976. A swinging twenty-five year old, Brown drove a bus in Rainier, Oregon and wasn't averse to relationships with coworkers, although she pointedly snubbed mechanic Steven Heflin. Under police questioning and during a local search for the missing woman, Heflin stood out for his nervousness and bizarre behavior, and witnesses mentioned shots fired at 6:45 the previous evening and a truck departing the crime scene at roughly that time. The witness' description matched Heflin, and police obtained a warrant for his truck and home.

The truck was stained with blood in multiple locations — the bed, the bed liner, the bench seat — and more blond hairs were found there, as well. His home yielded gloves and a motorcycle jacket, both so recently cleaned they were still wet. Police also found a .22 Ruger revolver, the grip stained with something sticky, and a blood-stained shovel nearby.

Analysis showed the blood to be type O with positive Rh factors, a pattern common to 42% of the U.S. population, including Heflin. But the shovel and stains in the bus barn also contained protein C factors that Heflin's blood didn't have. Unfortunately, all this proved was that someone else's blood besides Heflin's was involved, as Vicki Brown's blood type was not known. The yanked-out hair was matched to hairs from her brush, but not with scientific certainty.

With nothing else to go on, police gave the Ruger revolver to Herbert MacDonnell, who wrote the book on blood spatter analysis but was also highly competent in other forensic fields. MacDonnell found that C-factor blood had not only spattered the Ruger's exterior, presumably as the bullet struck the victim; it had actually been sucked into the barrel, probably as the hot gasses cooled and contracted after it had been fired. While backspatter isn't uncommon (blood will splash about), a .22 has a small barrel; it seemed logical that the barrel had to be close to the victim's bare skin for the blood to be sucked inside.

Through a series of tests, conducted on fatally diseased and dying animals, MacDonnell prepared a table of how much blood was sucked how far into the Ruger's barrel when the revolver was fired at various distances from both bare and clothed skin. His final conclusion was three inches from bare skin and perhaps less, with the head being the most likely target. When Brown refused Heflin's latest advances, he attacked and pistol-whipped her, then hauled her up against the wall and shot her in the face.

Heflin was convicted of murder and sentenced to death, although his sentence was commuted to life imprisonment. Vicki Brown's body was never found.

Shotgun accident? (1981)

Although attorney Martin Dillon suspected his wife, Patricia, was having an affair with his best friend and her employer, Dr. Stephen Scher, the two men's friendship rolled along. On June 2, they went skeet shooting together in Montrose, Pennsylvania, and as the day was ending, Dillon spotted a porcupine and took off running toward it, Scher's 16-gauge pump-action shotgun, loaded with buckshot, in hand. But his booklace was untied and when he was roughly 250 feet away from Scher and out of sight, Dillon tripped, landing on the shotgun. It went off and killed him.

Scher investigated the shot, found his friend, and being a medical doctor, attempted CPR despite the gaping, scalloped hole in Dillon's chest, covering himself with blood in the attempt. It was of course a useless gesture. Scher then took his temper out on the shotgun. In front of a witness, he swung the 16-gauge against a tree, smashing it so, as he put it, it could never kill again.

Autopsy by a local doctor confirmed the gaping,

1.5 x 1 inch oval wound with scalloped edges had been the direct cause of Dillon's death (as if there had been any doubt). Powder burns were reported around the injury. Dillon's boot lace indeed was untied. The death was ruled accidental and the case closed.

But several skeptics weren't content, and the most vocal and persistent of these was the victim's father, Lawrence Dillon, the mayor of Montrose. Remembering the rumors of an affair between Scher and Patricia Dillon, he pressed for an investigation. When Scher moved to South Carolina, only for Patricia to follow and marry him, Dillon père's insistence intensified. But local authorities refused to bow to pressure, even from the mayor, and no investigation followed.

Another skeptic was the police officer who documented the scene of the shooting, Trooper Francis Zanin. He believed it looked staged and took his photographs very carefully. One problem was the untied bootlace. The boot top had not loosened, as it would have if Dillon had been running, but instead remained snug against his leg. Dillon's pant leg was hiked up above his boots, as if he'd been crouching rather than running. Various blood-stained objects were found close to the body, including not only Dillon's shooting goggles and protective "earmuff" headgear, which he might have carried with him if he'd taken off after a sudden game target, but also several unbroken clay pigeons, which he wouldn't have. Blood had splashed the goggles and earmuffs, but Dillon's face was clean where those would have been worn. And who loaded heavy, #4 buckshot for skeet shooting?

But for twelve years the investigation remained dormant, with local prosecutors not entirely convinced of Scher's innocence but believing no case could be built against him. Finally in 1988, Lawrence Dillon hired a law enforcement official turned forensic reconstructionist, Warren Stewart Bennett. He agreed to examine the evidence and re-create the death scene.

Bennett wisely chose to concentrate on the fatal wound. According to Scher's story, Dillon tripped, fell on the gun, and accidentally shot himself, implying a contact shot. But a 16-gauge shotgun has a round barrel roughly two-thirds of an inch across. For the resulting wound to be 1 x 1.5 inches, the pellets had to have spread out. Scalloping is another indication of that spreading, which happens at some point after the pellets exit the barrel. The question became, how far away must the barrel's mouth have been from Dillon's chest to cause that particular wound?

The answer, found through Bennett's testing, was a bombshell. The shotgun had to have been somewhere between three to five feet away from Dillon when it went off. The scalloping and blood spatter on Dillon's trousers indicated it was held above him at roughly a forty-five degree angle — not below him, as it would have been if he'd fallen on it.

Examination of the other evidence found not only blood on the boots Scher had worn that day, but also blood spatter. He was much nearer Dillon than the 250 feet he'd claimed. There was blood on Dillon's boots, too, as if he'd been sitting or crouching when shot, not running.

Over Patricia Scher's objections, in 1995 Lawrence Dillon finally succeeded in having his son's body exhumed for another autopsy, this one performed by Dr. Isidore Mihalakis. Another bombshell hit: Dr. Mihalakis could find no trace of powder burns in Dillon's skin, proving it was not a contact shot that killed him, and he declared it an obvious homicide.

On the stand, Scher admitted his entire story was a twenty-year-old lie. He and Dillon had argued over Patricia, he said, then they'd fought over the shotgun and it had accidentally gone off. But when killed, Dillon was wearing earplugs, which some repetitive shooters (skeet, trap, target) wear beneath shooting earmuffs for additional hearing protection. Dillon could not have heard Scher, much less argued with him.

Figure 44 Live-fire qualification aboard USS *Enterprise*, with both shooter and examiner wearing proper "earmuff" protection.

Scher was convicted of murder and sentenced to life without parole. Although an appeals court briefly overturned the verdict, the Pennsylvania Supreme Court reversed that decision and returned Scher to prison.

A Tribute to Peace Officers

by "Scotty"

Known by the colorful name of "Thief Takers" as far back as 16th century England, this band of men, organized by Sir Robert Peel in the early 19th century, evolved into the present day highly-organized entity needed to preserve the establishment of order in today's increasingly crowded society. In America the first steps in establishing a law enforcement organization were taken in 1631 by Boston and spread to all 13 colonies. Unpaid and part-time, officers were called "The Night Watch." In 1712 again Boston lead the way in hiring the first full-time, paid peace officers in all 13 colonies.

We have evolved from primitive bounty hunters to officers with hundreds of hours' training in many disciplines. Also they're equipped with a level of advanced electronic gear unheard of just a few short years ago.

How many of us have attended the graduation ceremony of a young, eager recruit and felt pride at their decision to stay the rigorous course, proving their resolve and commitment. Sparkling and shining in their new uniforms, they await their futures.

That future will inevitably record split-second life-or-death decisions. In that fiery crucible will their deepest core beliefs be tested as never before. Conscience and training will be weighed in the balance of milliseconds that will seem like eternity. Moments when everything goes as planned, and moments when everything goes terribly wrong. The dates listed here are but a fraction of the all-too-many that compose the immutable history of law enforcement. The acronym EOW has become all too familiar: end of watch.

- **May 17, 1792:** New York City, first recorded death of a lawman killed in the line of duty.
- **April 14, 1865:** In one of history's greatest ironies, President Lincoln approved the formation of what is now the U.S. Secret Service. On that same day John Wilkes Booth fired the fatal shot.
- **April 1, 1878–April 28, 1881:** Six lawmen die at the hands of outlaw Billy the Kid.
- **May 6, 1886:** Eight Chicago officers died during the Haymarket Riot.
- **December 15, 1890:** Eight officers serving with the U.S. Bureau of Indian Affairs died while on duty.
- **1916:** Anna Hart became the first female law enforcement officer killed in the line of duty.
- **1930:** The single deadliest year in law enforcement history, with 282 officers killed.
- **January 2, 1932:** Six lawmen died during the Young Brothers Massacre.
- **April 6, 1970:** Four California Highway Patrolmen died in the Newhall Incident, which echoed throughout the entire law enforcement community. The result was major reforms in training procedures, firearms, and arrest techniques.
- **September 11, 2001:** The deadliest day in law enforcement history. 72 officers died while on duty.

Apart from the military, no other career presents such risks or requires such crucial decision-making skills. The inevitable question arises, why would anyone choose a career with such risks? Money and fame would definitely not be motivating factors. Each applicant must ponder and weigh the odds inherent in wearing a uniform against the everyday risks faced by untrained civilians.

By contrast, police academies have set high standards, often required by law, to ensure that officers are trained to handle every known situation, as well as being ready to expect the unexpected.

On that Tuesday morning the day shift had begun much like every other day. The good-natured bantering at roll call was a time-honored tradition, almost a requirement, as the veterans knew how much it helped in facing the day. After all, New York City can be hectic with its restless tide of humanity. There is bound to be some friction, some disagreements, some consequences all the way from a shouting match between egos to the ultimate tragedy of a life ending violently and too soon.

On this seemingly ordinary day, the hand of fate would choose 72 officers from several different agencies to give their all in serving their fellow man. It was the 11th day of September, a day forever stained with the blood of those 72 officers. Today, it's simply referred to as 9/11.

Part of America died that day, part of you and me. While we cannot erase history's checkerboard of nights and days, we can honor the living. A simple "Thank you," spoken to an officer, can be more of a gift than we realize. Or a simple card just to show that we are fellow travelers, and not contestants in a senseless adversarial game of chance. That officer may save your life tomorrow by issuing a citation for speeding or other common violation. Or their life may be weighed in the balance while rescuing you from a hostage situation.

The goal is not a perfect, crime free society. Instead, millions of citizens will sleep safe in their beds tonight because somewhere those sentinels are holding that thin blue line steady and intact during the often lonely hours of the night shift. They serve on a battlefield just as real as the one soldiers encounter in warfare. Although times may change, the same minefields exist. We can do no less than pray for their protection and safety as they minister to us.

References

Evans, Colin. The Casebook of Forensic Detection: How Science Solved 100 of the World's Most Baffling Crimes. New York: John Wiley & Sons, Inc., 1996.

Evans, Colin. *Murder 2: The Second Casebook of Forensic Detection.* New York: John Wiley & Sons, Inc., 2004.

Hamby, James E., PhD, and James W. Thorpe, PhD. "The History of Firearm Identification," in *The Association of Firearm and Tool Mark Examiners Journal,* 30th Anniversary Issue, Volume 31 Number 3, Summer 1999 and reprinted in full with permission on www.FirearmsID.com.

Indiana State Police Laboratory Division. "Forensic Firearms Identification Unit Test Methods," on www.IN.gov.

National Institute of Justice. "Firearm Examiner Training," on www.NIJ.gov.

Ramsland, Katherine M. *Inside the Minds of Healthcare Serial Killers: Why They Kill.* Westport, Connecticut: Praeger Publishers, 2007, viewed on www.GoogleBooks.com.

Reed, Barry C. "The Sacco-Vanzetti Case: The Trial of the Century," in American Bar Association Journal, Volume 46, page 867, August 1960, viewed on www.GoogleBooks.com.

Rudin, Norah and Keith Inman. "The Forensic Science Timeline," on www.ForensicDNA.com.

Unknown. "Detection of Crime by Photography," originally published in *Chamber's Journal,* December 30, 1893, reprinted by George Mason University, Center for History and New Media, on chnm.gmu.edu.

Unknown. *Firearms History, Technology & Development,* on www.FirearmsHistory.Blogspot.com.

Watson, Bruce. *Sacco and Vanzetti: The Men, the Murders, and the Judgment of Mankind.* New York: Viking Penguin, 2007, viewed on www.GoogleBooks.com.

List of illustrations

Cover

Close-up of an M9 semi-auto pistol, taken by Cpl. Kurt Fredrickson of the U.S. military.

Theory

Cutaway of ammunition cartridge, by Pearson Scott Foresman.

Centerfire vs. rimfire firing pin marings on expended shell casings, from the FBI.gov website.

Rifling inside the barrel of a Marlin .35 Remington, by Wikimedia Commons contributor Rickochet.

Timeline:

Fire-spear wielder and an early form of manual grenade launcher.

Ribauldequin, drawn by Leonardo Da Vinci.

Diagram of the flintlock mechanism, by Pearson Scott Foresman.

1840 advertisement for the 1836 Colt single-action revolver.

1854 Adams double-action revolver, by Wikimedia Commons contributor Harryvc.

Civil War era Minié balls of several calibers, by Wikimedia Commons contributor Mike Cumpston.

World War II era Thompson submachine gun with box magazine.

Types

Bowen Classic Arms 500 Linebaugh revolver, by
Wikimedia Commons user Mike Cumpston.

Revolver cylinder extended and partially loaded, by
the Hong Kong Police Force.

Half and full moon clips, by Wikimedia Commons
user Krd.

Shell casing being ejected by M14 rifle during target
practice aboard USS Ronald Reagan, by Phan
Christine Singh.

U.S. Navy sailor inserting a fresh magazine into M9
pistol during target practice aboard USS Boxer,
by Trevor Welsh.

FN P90 bullpup, carried by a Cypriot National
Guardsman during a parade in Lamaca, by
Wikimedia Commons contributor eLNuko.

Combat-ready SA80 bullpup assault rifle, by Lance
Corporal R.L. Kugler, Jr.

12-gauge shotgun shell with transparent plastic
casing, by Wikimedia Commons user Lax1.

Double-barrelled break-action shotgun, by
Wikimedia Commons user Commander Zulu.

Modern reproduction of the Winchester M1887 12-
gauge lever-action shotgun, by Wikimedia
Commons user Commander Zulu.

Armed Response Team member very capably holding
a 12-gauge Mossberg 500 tactical shotgun during
training aboard USS Dwight D. Eisenhower, by
Tracy Lee Didas.

12-gauge Brenneke shotgun slug, by Wikimedia
Commons user Lax1.

Full-metal jacketed cartridge for the .45, by
Wikimedia Commons user Malis.

9mm hollow-point cartridge, by Wikimedia Commons
user Jpogi.

12-gauge buckshot, by Wikimedia Commons user
Julien0540.

Caliber comparison. From left to right, 9mm Luger,

7.62mm, .357 SIG, 10mm, .40 S&W, .45 GAP, and .50 AE. By Wikimedia Commons user Spectrums.

Kimber Raptor .45ACP with NRA B-3 target, by Wikimedia Commons user Chaney44145.

Land to land, or groove to groove. Cropped image by Wikimedia Commons user Thuringius.

U.S. Marine carrying Winchester M97 shotgun in the Pacific Theater.

Examination

Beretta 8045 made for the LAPD, by Wikimedia Commons user Age ranger.

Fired bullet with flattened nose and clear striations beside unfired bullet, from Tony Orr.

Shattered and warped recovered bullets, from FBI.gov.

Technician using a comparison microscope, from FBI.gov.

Polygonal vs. normal rifling, by Wikimedia Commons user Fluzwup.

.38 hollow-point bullet, showing typical mushrooming and visible striations, by Wikimedia Commons user Rickochet.

Positive identification of a questioned bullet, from FBI.gov.

Centerfire vs. rimfire firing pin marings on expended shell casings, from the FBI.gov website.

Positive identification on breech face markings, from FBI.gov.

Cases:

Sacco and Vanzetti wearing handcuffs.

Colt 1903 Pocket Hammerless, by Wikimedia Commons user Asams10.

Field-stripped Walther P99, showing interchangeable

barrel, by Wikimedia Commons user Hrd10.
Sailors aboard USS Enterprise wearing shooter's
earmuffs during target practice, by Milosz
Reterski.

About the Author

Hi, I'm Gunnar Grey. I write books. I'm a historian, a forensics nut, a target shooter, and a retired adventurer and equestrian. I read avidly and post reviews or at least ratings for most of the books I read. In addition, I format ebooks for myself and a few clients. If you need an ebook formatted or want to meet my references, check out my blog, Mysteries and Histories.

I live in Humble, Texas, just north of Houston, with four parakeets, the aforementioned husband (who's even more entertaining than the birds), a fig tree, a vegetable garden, the lawn from the bad place, three armloads of potted plants, and a coffee maker that's likely the most important item we own.

Also by J. Gunnar Grey

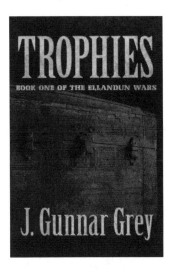

Chapter One

current time

Three neat entry wounds drilled through the silk of Aunt Edith's blouse, stiffened and blackened by crusted blood. The underlying color was unrecognizable. I only knew it was supposed to be green because she wore it during our unfriendly dinner the previous evening and I remembered. Lying on the sidewalk with her legs crumpled beneath her, she seemed even tinier than normal, like a toy that had been roughly played with and then pitched aside.

I dropped to my knees beside her. Her eyes were wide, staring at the dawn breaking beyond the storefronts, and her mouth gaped. She was such a private person, so contained, elegant, brilliant as gold beside the base metals of the rest of us. Death seemed an exposure, a stripping of her secrets. A humiliation.

I reached out to stroke the drifting black and silver tendrils of her hair into place. But a hand snatched my wrist and twisted it aside. I jerked my head up—

—the picture window of the Carr Gallery, just overhead, was splattered with something dark. More of it sprayed the polished maple door, the brass railing and handle and mail slot. A small hole in the door, at waist level, had been marked with chalk—

—more dark stains, lit obliquely by the dawn light, trickled down the red brick, dripped from one concrete step to the next, painted the sidewalk. I suddenly realized I could smell it—

—I ignored the background *crump* of artillery fire and panned the rifle's scope along the enemy emplacement, atop the ridge overlooking our sand-bagged trench. Beneath the camouflage netting and wilting tree branches I made out one big field gun with its muzzle recoiling, another, a third—

—the enemy spotter stood contemptuously in full view, binoculars to his eyes, gazing off to my left but sweeping this way. The rangefinder showed the distance at eight hundred meters. I set the elevation turret and aligned the sight's upper chevron on his center of mass, drifting aside by one hash mark to compensate for the gentle flow of air across my right cheek. Binocular lenses flashed sunsparks. His lips moved as I took up the initial pressure on the trigger—

—flashback with visual, auditory, tactile, and olfactory hallucinations. Hadn't happened in months. It was impossible to prevent it, stop it, tone it down, or predict its arrival. But we were intimate enemies, my flashback and I, and I knew its script. I clenched every muscle I possessed, including my eyes, and froze in place, ignoring it all. It's how I'd taught myself to respond when the city street morphed into a battlefield without warning, and so far it had prevented anyone from locking me up. I was even able to fool most acquaintances into thinking I was still sane.

But nothing blocked the sights, sounds, or other manifestations. Machine gun fire hammered into the nonexistent sandbags, thuds echoing in my bones, and the dust and acrid gunpowder caught at the back of my throat. Someone screamed, a long shrill sound that climbed higher in pitch and volume, scraping across my nerves. The enemy guns chattered again and a fire of agony spurted across my back. Wavery, sick-feeling blackness rushed in behind the pain. I refused to wobble. I ignored the war zone and the adrenaline tearing me apart, and waited for the screaming in my damaged memory to stop. For several more seconds it dragged on, a horrible rising shriek, but finally it cut out in its usual abrupt manner, as if someone hit a neurological mute button.

The flashback lost. It couldn't control my actions nor force me to betray my internal damage to the civilians. I wanted to collapse with relief. I refused to do that, too.

Ambient city noises resumed. There were lots of voices around, both live ones and the scratchy overlay of radio transmissions, and in the distance someone called my name. Even with my eyes squeezed tight, popping emergency lights strobed across my retinas. I still smelled the blood.

I failed Aunt Edith. Everything inside me wrenched. I failed her and now she's dead. That particular fear, of failing someone important, always followed the flashback. Knowing it was coming never prevented the reaction. I wouldn't show that, either.

Only when I knew I was back in real time did I open my eyes.

Dawn and Boston had returned. The battlefield was gone, replaced by the street of upscale shops, converted from historic red-brick row houses. Picture windows with discreet painted logos and black wrought-iron bars alternated with concrete steps rising to entries, each landing decorated with trees or flowers in wooden barrels. Blood painted the steps and façade of the Carr Gallery, Aunt Edith lay dead and hidden beside the entryway stairs, and there on her other side was a doughy face like something a baker played with before rolling it out. Its expression was outraged and the hand attached to the equally doughy body still gripped my wrist, our arms crossing above Aunt Edith's neck.

"Don't muck up my crime scene, man," he said in pure Brooklynese.

Ice clogged my veins. My field of vision constricted until all I could see was his face before me. I could control my physical behavior during the flashback and even my awareness, once I realized its game was on; I couldn't chain the emotions, nor the adrenaline. The muscles I'd released tautened again. Flight wasn't an option, but pounding something was. "She's not a crime scene."

He glanced down, as if only then realizing Aunt Edith was, or had been, human. "She is now."

I went for him. But strong arms hauled me back and away.

One of the live voices sniggered in my ear. "What a circus."

No sense fighting. It wasn't the policemen restraining me nor the crime scene technician I wanted to pound. I wanted the spotter, the one that got away during the war. If I could find the murderer who'd dossed down my Aunt Edith, he'd do, as well.

"Charles!"

That was my cousin Patricia's voice, piercing the enshrouding mental fog. I ignored the hands gripping me and peered over my shoulder. She stood alone, makeup smeared and lipstick chewed off, in the midst of the curious bystanders behind a strip of yellow tape. Flimsy as it looked, that tape represented the boundaries of the permissible and therefore was sufficient to stop her. Had they put that up behind me? I couldn't remember seeing it, much less ducking beneath it.

Patty seemed safe, so I turned back to Aunt Edith and eased from the policemen's holds. But a man stepped between the crime scene technician and me — between Aunt Edith and me. "Mr. Ellandun?"

I looked around him and didn't bother being subtle about it. Aunt Edith stared back, the heavy emptiness of the dead replacing her usual honest and level gaze, neither judgmental nor compassionate, with something blank. One of her pumps had fallen off and a chalk circle had been drawn around it. A bit of trash; the most amazing woman I'd ever met, and she'd been tossed aside like a bit of trash. It was beyond wrong. It was obscene.

"It's captain, actually," I said. "Captain Charles Ellandun."

He kept speaking, but as usual, Aunt Edith dominated the scene without trying. Only now it wasn't her elegant vivacity accomplishing that feat, but its absence. She had been the Rock of Gibraltar in my life since I'd been eleven and meeting her had been the watershed moment of my watershed year. She'd always been vital, compelling, more alive than the city itself. It was impossible for her to be dead.

Her skirt was the same as last night, as well, woven wool in the Hunter tartan plaid, the one she'd worn the day I first met her. Likely she'd returned to the art gallery directly after dinner, then. She still wore her wedding ring, as usual her only jewelry. There was no sign of her purse.

"Captain?" It was the man who'd stepped between us, a plainclothes detective in a button-down shirt and dark slacks.

Pounding him wouldn't help, either. I forced myself to look at him. I even remembered his question, although I was too distracted to focus. "Yes, I own several handguns."

"And were you in the war?" His voice was professional, beautifully modulated, and easy to listen to, even at that moment.

Even if he was an irritant.

"Yes." Was I ever.

The long, drawn-out *skrip* of a closing zipper demolished all my good intentions. The doughy crime

111

scene technician slowly sealed the body bag. The shadow of the canvas flaps fluttered across her blank eyes. Then she vanished inside.

The air left my lungs as if I no longer needed oxygen, either. Again tunnel vision narrowed my field of focus, this time to the gurney as it rumbled past. The technician's hand rested atop the lumpy canvas.

I yearned to go for him again and fought the flashback-induced impulse. Although the battlefield had vanished into the scattered recesses of my mind, the subconscious, primal scream of combat still goaded me. Then I caught up with what the irritant standing beside me had just said in his elegant tenor.

Where were you last night.

I stared at him while the implications of that question soaked into the corners of my damaged brain. How long that took, while we locked eyes and assessed each other, I don't know; accurately measuring time has never been one of my finer accomplishments. But the details of his perfect face — expensively styled bronze-toned hair rippling above his ears, brown eyes steady and suspicious, smooth tan that had nothing to do with working outside, not a trace of stubble on the square jaw — left an afterimage on my retinas like the strobing emergency lights. How could he stand being so damned perfect? It didn't matter whether pounding him would help or not. I went for him instead.

Again hands hauled me back. And suddenly cousin Patricia was between us, grabbing handfuls of my sport shirt and shaking me, or at least it. "Charles, for God's sake, what is *wrong* with you?"

I nearly told her, nearly reminded her of my diagnosis, but couldn't see the point even if I was an Ellandun and lived for the fight. The gurney and the moment were gone and the bloody adrenaline finally snapped. I shuddered beneath her clenched fists as the aftereffects kicked in. From the way her already wide green eyes were stretching wider, she felt it, too.

"Charles?" This time, her voice was less than a whisper and it broke in the middle of my name.

If I could have stopped the shaking, to protect Patty I would have done it. I'd failed her, too, and again I closed my eyes. Whatever showed in my all-too-transparent face, she didn't need to see it.

Because I'd tried to tackle a plainclothes police detective, Boston's finest slung me into the back of a squad car to cool down, one of an armload of emergency vehicles scattered about the street. They closed the doors, too, and how the July heat that rapidly built up inside that car was supposed to help me cool down, I cannot imagine. The interior stank from the stale fast-food wrappers littering the floorboards and the stain of something I didn't want to identify on the part of the seat I avoided.

I'd put up with all of it if I could have Aunt Edith back. She couldn't possibly be dead.

Outside the patrol car and a few yards away, Patricia and Brother Perfect chatted like old friends, her eyes sliding sideways to check on me every minute or so, his never leaving her damp and smudged face. He'd positioned her so she couldn't see the blood. Her mousy brown hair strained back in a knot that looked painted on, but then so did her jeans, and with her streamlined figure, I'm certain the average male never noticed the hair. To give him credit, Brother Perfect's gaze didn't drop, not even to her green cotton camp shirt, halfway unbuttoned from the bottom and tied in a knot above her belt buckle. Perhaps the stained handkerchief she used to rearrange the sad remnants of her makeup put him off.

Finally she walked away, ducked beneath the yellow crime-scene tape, and waited outside the perimeter, staring at me in the back of the squad car with her lower lip between her teeth. Brother Perfect watched her until their eyes met for a brief glance, and then he turned, opened the squad car door, and slid into the front passenger seat.

To give him further credit, he didn't bother scolding me. "You say you have several guns. Tell me about them."

I rubbed my eyes. "I own an M-16, a Mauser sniper's rifle—"

"Handguns, Captain. Tell me about your handguns."

To hell with him. I moved over until I breathed the outside air. "I have a Colt .45, two old Walther nine millimeters and two new ones—"

"What's the smallest bore handgun you own?"

The question threw me until I realized the holes in Aunt Edith's lungs had been small. "The nine millimeters."

"No twenty-two?" he asked. "Nothing smaller than a nine?"

"No," I said.

He stared at me for a long moment. The shakes had diminished as the adrenaline ebbed away, leaving me taut and intensely aware, and the skeptical curl of his lip made his opinion of my veracity perfectly clear. Again my temper began heating — there was something about him that made that a delightful process — but I swore this time I'd hang onto my self-control.

"I've kept records," I said. "And my LTC Class A and FID are both in order. You're welcome to check them."

"Thank you." The tone of his voice left no doubt he'd do so whether I volunteered them or not. "Are you carrying now?"

"No." But I intended to rectify that as soon as possible.

"So where were you last night?"

"At home." I gave him the address of my condo on the waterfront, north of Burroughs Wharf and well away from the tourist congestion at the Aquarium and Rowe's Wharf. He didn't write anything down; perhaps he had a photographic memory. "I had dinner with

Aunt Edith around seven, got home around nine thirty or a bit after, and stayed in."

She had tried to persuade me to be sociable and forgiving, get involved with her latest bloody art show, see the family while everyone was in town as if I had a particle of interest whatsoever in them. The remembrance of how little encouragement I had given her during that, our final conversation, set my insides squirming.

"Can anyone confirm that?"

I hadn't even checked email. "No."

That internal squirming had a distinctly frigid tinge to it now. He'd gun for motive next; wasn't that how they did it on those stupid cop shows?

But he surprised me by motioning me out of the car. He leaned atop the hood, his perfect face strobed by the popping emergency lights so that he seemed dipped in blood then wiped clean, over and over again. I knew that image would stay in my nightmares for a long time to come. Something else to appreciate about the man.

"Don't leave town," he said, and walked away.

J. Gunnar Grey

δ

Dingbat Publishing
Humble, Texas

Made in the USA
San Bernardino, CA
26 April 2015